SIMPLE SENTENCES, SUBSTITUTION, AND INTUITIONS

Simple Sentences, Substitution, and Intuitions

JENNIFER SAUL

OXFORD
UNIVERSITY PRESS

P
295
.S28
2007

OXFORD
UNIVERSITY PRESS

Great Clarendon Street, Oxford OX2 6DP

Oxford University Press is a department of the University of Oxford.
It furthers the University's objective of excellence in research, scholarship,
and education by publishing worldwide in

Oxford New York

Auckland Cape Town Dar es Salaam Hong Kong Karachi
Kuala Lumpur Madrid Melbourne Mexico City Nairobi
New Delhi Shanghai Taipei Toronto

With offices in

Argentina Austria Brazil Chile Czech Republic France Greece
Guatemala Hungary Italy Japan Poland Portugal Singapore
South Korea Switzerland Thailand Turkey Ukraine Vietnam

Oxford is a registered trade mark of Oxford University Press
in the UK and in certain other countries

Published in the United States
by Oxford University Press Inc., New York

© Jennifer Saul 2007

British Library Cataloguing in Publication Data

Data available

Library of Congress Cataloging in Publication Data

Saul, Jennifer Mather, 1968–
Simple sentences, substitution, and intuitions / Jennifer Saul.
p. cm.
Includes bibliographical references and index.
ISBN-13: 978–0–19–921915–5 (alk. paper)
ISBN-10: 0–19–921915–X (alk. paper)
1. Grammar, Comparative and general—Sentences. 2. Language and languages—Philosophy.
3. Semantics (Philosophy) I. Title.
P295.S28 2007
415—dc22   2006103222

Typeset by Laserwords Private Limited, Chennai, India
Printed in Great Britain
on acid-free paper by
Biddles Ltd., King's Lynn, Norfolk

ISBN 978–0–19–921915–5

1 3 5 7 9 10 8 6 4 2

To Ray Drainville and to Julie and Frank Saul, with love

Contents

Preface

It has long been thought that co-referential names (like 'Superman' and 'Clark Kent') appear to be freely substitutable without change of truth value in simple sentences like (1) and (1*), but not in sentences containing certain special constructions, like (2) and (2*).

(1) Superman flies.
(1*) Clark flies.
(2) Lois believes that Superman flies.
(2*) Lois believes that Clark flies.

Most authors have taken this appearance at face value, and offered explanations of the differences between sentences of these types. Even those who deny that substitution really does fail in (2) and (2*) agree that we need to explain the apparent differences between sentences that do and do not contain expressions like 'believes'—the so-called 'opacity-producing' constructions that are standardly blamed for substitution failure.

   In Saul (1997*a*), I challenged this picture by presenting examples like (3) and (3*), in which substitution failure seems to occur even in what I called 'simple sentences'—those lacking the standard opacity-producing constructions:

(3) Clark Kent went into the phone booth and Superman came out.
(3*) Superman went into the phone booth and Clark Kent came out.

I argued that the debate over substitution has been shaped by a misunderstanding of the data in need of explanation: we cannot carve out a group of constructions that seem to give rise to substitution failure and treat them as a special case. Moreover, I suggested that these observations have important consequences for semantic theorising.

   At the time of my original paper, and for some time afterwards, I was convinced that the main significance of apparent substitution failures in simple sentences was for substitution puzzle cases such as those involving propositional attitude reports. More recently, it has become increasingly clear to me that they show something of wider interest than this: the most important lesson to come out of reflecting on simple sentences is a methodological one concerning the role of intuitions in philosophy of language. In particular, I have become convinced that they show traditional approaches to truth-conditional intuitions to be inadequate. (A terminological note: I use the phrase 'truth-conditions' to refer to the truth values of a sentence in a context, evaluated both at the actual world and at other possible worlds. Truth-conditional intuitions are intuitions about these truth values.)

In this book, my main purpose is to draw out this methodological lesson. Simple sentences serve as a kind of case study for this lesson. I argue that simple sentences help to show the failure of a certain sort of traditional methodological picture. This picture begins from the (relatively uncontroversial) thought that truth-conditional intuitions are an important source of data for philosophers of language. The fact that two sentences intuitively differ in truth value (in the same context) is taken to be good evidence that these sentences differ semantically—that they express different propositions. If sentence A is intuitively true and sentence B is intuitively false, then ideally one's semantic theory should give the result that A expresses a true proposition and B a false one. Of course, things are not always so ideal. Obviously, our intuitions sometimes go wrong. What B actually expresses may be true, and yet we may nonetheless judge it to be false. The standard way to explain such errors is to suggest that the source of our judgment may instead be some other proposition—which *is* false—that an utterance of B manages (either generally, or in some particular context) to convey to us. For example, a theorist who holds that an utterance of, 'Someone threw a grenade and I got hit', is true even if the speaker was the thrower needs to explain why it is that many will take the utterance to be false under these circumstances. They may do so by arguing that the intuition of falsehood is due to the falsehood of the conveyed (perhaps conversationally implicated) claim that someone *other than the speaker* threw the grenade.

Truth-conditional intuitions, then, are standardly dealt with in one of two ways:

1. By giving theories on which the intuitive truth conditions for sentences match their actual truth conditions.
2. By explaining why the intuitive truth conditions are incorrect. This standardly takes the form of pointing to conveyed propositions whose truth conditions do match the truth conditions we intuitively assign.

Simple sentences that seem to exhibit substitution failure show these options for accommodating intuitions to be inadequate. I argue for this by exploring various options for accommodating simple sentence intuitions within the traditional methodology, showing that they all fail. Next, I begin a process of trying to identify the assumptions that give rise to this failure. Eventually I am in a position to argue that simple sentences show the need for a means of accommodating truth-conditional intuitions which makes no use of what I call intuition-matching propositions: propositions whose truth conditions match those indicated by our intuitions.

Once we look beyond intuition-matching propositions, it becomes apparent that there are potential ways of accommodating intuitions that have failed to receive the attention they deserve. In particular, results from psychology help to show that there are many ways our intuitions might err that have nothing to do with our grasping intuition-matching propositions. In the case of simple sentences, there are data that render very appealing an explanation that draws on cognitive architecture and processing considerations. I develop this explanation, showing that it holds great promise for explaining our intuitions about these sentences.

Psychological explanations of intuitions, like those suggested here, have a great deal of as-yet-unexplored promise for philosophy of language. If the arguments of this book are right, philosophers of language have unduly limited themselves when considering ways that truth-conditional intuitions may go wrong. They have failed to explore options that do not involve intuition-matching propositions, and they have failed to explore empirical literature that may bear on these other options. Once these options are explored, apparently intractable problems may turn out to be far more amenable to solution: for example, perhaps the reason neither pragmatic nor semantic solutions to substitution puzzles have proven successful is that a psychological explanation is called for instead.

CHAPTERS

Chapter 1, Substitution and Simple Sentences, is a detailed look at the consequences of apparent substitution failures in simple sentences for standard debates on substitution. It begins with a look at propositional attitude-reporting substitution puzzles and traditional approaches to these puzzles. This serves as a good illustration of the traditional method-ology discussed above, but it also allows us to see the seriousness of the problems simple sentence puzzle cases pose for standard approaches to substitution.

Chapter 2, Simple Sentences and Semantics, examines attempts by Graeme Forbes, Joseph Moore, David Pitt, and Stefano Predelli to develop semantic theories on which anti-substitution intuitions about simple sentences are actually correct. Chapter 3, Simple Sentences and Implicatures, examines attempts (like Alex Barber's) to explain away anti-substitution intuitions as due to conversational implicatures. I argue that all of these attempts fail, and that further attempts along similar lines will also fail. The most important problems that I raise are ones that arise in one form or another for all of the views discussed: (a) the Enlightenment Problem: they need to make implausible claims about the states of mind of conversational participants; and (b) the Aspect Problem: they make use of theoretically problematic entities. These problems will serve to motivate my alternative approach to truth-conditional intuitions.

Chapters 4 and 5 explore what will be needed to deal adequately with the Enlightenment Problem and the Aspect Problem. Chapter 4 begins my diagnosis of the Enlightenment Problem with 'A problematic assumption'. I begin by noting that theorists have tended to proceed as if they adhere to a principle that I call *Expressed or Implicated* (EOI):

Expressed or Implicated (EOI): For an utterance of a sentence *S* in a context *C*, the truth-conditional intuitions of competent, rational speakers who are relevantly well-informed must match the truth conditions of either what is (semantically) expressed or what is implicated by *S* in *C*.

This chapter argues that (EOI) is false, and attempts to diagnose why it is that theorists have tended to proceed as though they accepted it. Chapter 5 begins by exploring what would be needed to fully evade the Enlightenment Problem, arguing for the abandonment not only of (EOI), but also of some important variants of (EOI). Next, it considers what is required to avoid the Aspect Problem. By the end of this chapter, it is clear that philosophers of language need to develop theories on which truth-conditional intuitions may not be due to any proposition whose truth conditions match those indicated by the intuitions.

Chapter 6 shows how it is that we can abandon the traditional picture and develop theories like those Chapters 4 and 5 show to be needed. This chapter offers an account of simple sentences that makes no use of 'matching propositions', drawing instead on considerations of psychological processing. The explanation developed is, it seems to me, a very satisfying one. It also fits quite naturally both with widely accepted assumptions about cognitive architecture and with the relevant empirical data. In addition, it is compatible with a wide variety of views on the semantics of names.

Finally, I explore the methodological consequences of adopting an account like that suggested above. In particular, I explore a worry that one might have: that once we expand our intuition-explaining options to include psychological explanations as well as more traditional ones, it may become *too* easy to explain intuitions away. I suggest that this is not so. The availability of such an explanation in one area does not indicate that such explanations will always be available. Moreover, to fully and properly support a psychological explanation, empirical data are needed, which may or may not be forthcoming. Such explanations can also be disconfirmed by empirical data. As an illustration of this point, I discuss possible experiments that might bear on the viability of the psychological explanation offered in Chapter 6.

APPENDICES

Appendix A discusses terms other than names that seem to give rise to substitution puzzles. It is far from obvious how to extend other accounts to cover these cases, but the psychological explanation suggested in Chapter 6 could be easily extended to accommodate them.

Appendix B returns to the topic of propositional attitude reporting and substitution. In particular, it explores the implications for propositional attitude reporting of accepting an account like that offered in Chapter 6. I suggest that—even though the account is confined to simple sentences, and even though it is compatible with a variety of views on names—accepting it may pose difficulties for opponents of Millianism.

Acknowledgements

I am very grateful to all those who have helped with this book over the last few years—by reading parts of it, discussing the issues with me, or simply giving much-needed moral support. In particular, I would like to thank John Anderson, Kent Bach, Alex Barber, Josep Corbi, Nick Clarke, Graeme Forbes, Tobies Grimaltos, Rosanna Keefe, Steve Laurence, Steve Makin, Joe Moore, Marta Moreno, Carlos Moya, Eric Olson, Gary Ostertag, David Pitt, Stefano Predelli, Teresa Robertson, Julie and Frank Saul, Peter Smith, Jordi Valor, Ede Zimmerman, and some very helpful anonymous reviewers for Oxford University Press. I'd also like to thank audiences in Berlin, Cambridge, Nottingham, Portland, Sheffield, Valencia, and the Pacific and Eastern Division APAs for discussing material in this book with me. In addition, I'd like to thank Stan Fischer, who had nothing to do with this book but who introduced me to philosophy.

I'd like to single out David Braun and Chris Hookway for special thanks. Chris has given me huge amounts of much-needed encouragement and always been willing to discuss issues related to this book with me; his thoughts have helped to shape my thinking in important ways, and I can honestly say that this book would not have existed without his guidance. David and I developed an earlier version of the account offered in Chapter 6 (Braun and Saul 2002), and he has generously allowed me to draw on our joint paper for this book. In addition, he has gone far beyond the call of duty, reading and discussing pretty much every page of this book with me. I am deeply grateful for his willingness to do this—his help has vastly improved the book, although it would undoubtedly be yet more improved if I had taken all his advice.

I am extremely grateful to the AHRC and the Leverhulme Foundation for funding my work on this project (and, in the case of the Leverhulme, for funding so much else besides). I am also very grateful to Peter Momtchiloff for his help and to Albert Atkin, Jules Holroyd and Robin Scaife for excellent research assistance. I thank *Linguistics and Philosophy, Mind and Language,* and *Philosophical Studies* for permission to use material from work I have published in these journals; and Jenni Craig and Joy Mellor at OUP for all their their work on the book.

Finally, I want to thank Ray Drainville for supporting me both emotionally and intellectually through my work on this book, and through everything else, and for designing a beautiful cover which has made me view this book much more fondly; and to thank Theo Drainville-Saul for helping to entertain me through the final stages of this book.

1

Substitution and Simple Sentences

Simple sentences that seem to resist substitution pose serious problems for standard discussions of substitution puzzle cases. As indicated in the Preface, I take the main interest of these problems to lie in their broader methodological implications. Nonetheless, it is important to begin with a detailed look at substitution puzzle cases. This will help us to see how serious the problems posed by apparently substitution-resistant simple sentences are. And it will also give us a nice illustration of traditional approaches to accommodating truth-conditional intuitions. Since I take the ultimate lesson of simple sentences to be the need for new approaches to such intuitions, it will be helpful to have this in place as background.

A terminological reminder: as noted in the Preface, I use the phrase 'truth conditions' to refer to the truth values of a sentence in a context, evaluated both at the actual world and at other possible worlds. Truth-conditional intuitions are intuitions about these truth values.

1.1 SUBSTITUTION AND BELIEF REPORTING

1.1.1 Millianism, Fregeanism, and the problem of belief reports

An initially attractive view of names is that the sole semantic content of a name is the individual to whom it refers. (By 'semantic content of a name' I mean *contribution to the proposition semantically expressed* in a context by a sentence containing the name.) This view, Millianism, gains credence from the commonplace (though by no means unquestionable) thought that our goal in making assertions is to talk about the world—what we say in such assertions, it is reasonable to suppose, will be about things in the world; and when we use a name we simply say something about the individual named. So, according to this line of thought, it makes sense to assume that a name's semantic content will be simply its referent.[1] It also gains support from reflecting on some commonplace examples, like (1) and (1*), or (2) and (2*), below:

(1) Hesperus is a planet.
(1*) Phosphorus is a planet.
(2) Clark is thirsty.
(2*) Superman is thirsty.

Substituting 'Phosphorus' for 'Hesperus' in (1) to arrive at (1*) seems to make no difference to truth conditions. And the same seems true for the substitution of 'Superman' for 'Clark' in order to move from (2) to (2*).[2] The fact that co-referential names can be freely substituted in this way seems at first to lend support to the view that a name's sole semantic contribution—its sole contribution to the proposition expressed by a sentence containing it—is its reference.

But Millianism faces an important obstacle. Co-referential names do not seem freely substitutable in all sentences. In particular, it looks as though substitution of co-referential names can make a difference to truth conditions in sentences that report beliefs, such as (3) and (3*), or (4) and (4*) below.

(3) Helga believes that Hesperus is a planet.
(3*) Helga believes that Phosphorus is a planet.
(4) Lois believes that Clark is thirsty.
(4*) Lois believes that Superman is thirsty.

(3) seems as though it might be true even if (3*) is false; and (4) seems as though it might be true even if (4*) is false. Embedding a sentence within a belief report seems to have the result that co-referential names can no longer be freely substituted without change of truth conditions. And the same is true for other attitude verbs:

(5) Lois doubts that Clark is thirsty.
(5*) Lois doubts that Superman is thirsty.
(6) Lois fears that Clark is thirsty.
(6*) Lois fears that Superman is thirsty.

---

[1] This line of thought lends initial credibility to Millianism, but it is certainly not irresistible. Among other things, it moves rather quickly from reflections about what we say or assert to claims about semantic content.

[2] In the paragraph above, I discuss the truth values of *sentences*. Strictly speaking, only sentences in contexts have truth values. For convenience, I will sometimes use 'sentence' as shorthand for 'sentence in a context' or 'utterance of a sentence'. (Some theorists prefer to discuss sentences in contexts, while others prefer an utterance-based semantics. There are important issues here, but nothing in my discussion turns on this distinction.) Where contexts and utterances make a difference, I will discuss them explicitly.

Millianism on its own does not actually conflict with this.[3] However, a related theory, known as *Naïve Millianism* (the term is from Salmon 1986), does. According to the Naïve Millian, sentences that differ only in the substitution of one co-referential name for another must express the same proposition.[4] They must therefore have the same truth conditions. If (3), (4), (5) and (6) are true, then (3*), (4*), (5*), and (6*) must also be true.

Consideration of attitude-reporting sentences like those above has convinced many philosophers that a name's semantic content must at least sometimes be more than just its reference—Naïve Millianism must be false. Most famously, they have been important in convincing Fregeans that names have two semantic values, a sense and a reference.[5] A name's sense, for Frege, is a mode of presentation, or way of thinking, of its referent. Names like 'Hesperus' and 'Phosphorus', with the same reference, might nonetheless differ in sense. Frege maintained that the truth value of a sentence (which he took to be the sentence's reference) is compositionally determined by the references of its parts. Thus, (1) and (1*) must have the same truth value, as must (2) and (2*).

(1) Hesperus is a planet.
(1*) Phosphorus is a planet.
(2) Clark is thirsty.
(2*) Superman is thirsty.

These pairs do not, however, express the same propositions. The proposition expressed by a sentence is its sense, and it is determined compositionally by the senses of its parts. Propositions (or thoughts), made up of senses, are the objects of belief (and the other propositional attitudes). Thus, one might believe the proposition expressed by (1) without believing the proposition expressed by (1*). That is, one might believe that Hesperus is a planet without believing that Phosphorus is a planet. In other words, it should be possible for (3) and (3*) to differ in truth value.

(3) Helga believes that Hesperus is a planet.
(3*) Helga believes that Phosphorus is a planet.

---

[3] Mark Crimmins and John Perry's account (Crimmins and Perry 1989; Crimmins 1992), for example, is a Millian account on which (3) and (3*) and (4) and (4*) may differ in truth value. I discuss this account in § 1.1.3.1.

[4] Millians of course make an exception for sentences in which names are mentioned rather than used.

[5] The presentation of Frege's theory in the text above is of course an oversimplification. This oversimplified version is, I hope, adequate for my limited purposes.

But so far this is not possible. If truth value is compositionally determined by the references of a sentence's parts, and 'Hesperus' and 'Phosphorus' always refer to the same object, (3) and (3*) cannot not differ in truth value. To avoid this result, Frege maintained that in certain special contexts—such as within the embedded clause of a belief report—a term's customary sense becomes its reference. So in sentences like (3) and (3*) it is the senses of 'Hesperus' and 'Phosphorus' that are relevant to truth value. Because the senses are different, there is room for a difference in truth value between the two sentences, reflecting the fact that it seems possible for Helga to believe (1) without believing (1*).

Frege's view faces many well-known difficulties.[6] Nonetheless, most theorists remain convinced that Frege must be right at least in advocating a semantics that prevents substitution of co-referential names in belief reports and their ilk while allowing such substitution in other contexts.

1.1.2 Naïve Millians and implicature

Naïve Millians like Nathan Salmon (e.g. 1986) and Scott Soames (e.g. 1988), however, disagree. They maintain that co-referential names can be substituted for one another even in attitude-reporting sentences, without a change in truth conditions. The intuitions that seem to conflict with this claim, they maintain, are not quite what they seem. The way that they explain these intuitions provides a very nice illustration of the traditional methodology discussed in the preface. These intuitions, Naïve Millians maintain, are incorrect: they result from a certain sort of systematic and widespread error. More specifically, they result from a confusion between what is semantically expressed and what is pragmatically conveyed. We think that our intuitions are tracking semantic content—and so yielding correct results about the truth conditions of belief-reporting sentences—but this is not always the case. Instead, sometimes our intuitions reflect non-semantic features of belief-reporting sentences and utterances of them. Because we may not be sufficiently aware of the distinction between semantic and pragmatic elements of communication, and because even when we are aware of this distinction it can in practice be very difficult to draw, we are easily confused. When asked about the truth value of a belief-reporting sentence, then, we often go wrong—our judgments often reflect instead the truth value of some other claim somehow associated with the sentence in question.

---

[6] See, for example, Kripke (1972, 1988); Salmon (1981).

When it comes time to flesh this out more fully, Naïve theorists nearly invariably turn to Grice's theory of implicature.[7] Accordingly, we'll take a brief digression here to discuss Grice's theory in some detail. These details will become important later.

1.1.2.1 *Grice on implicature*

Grice's theory of implicature has been very important to the traditional methodology that I discussed in the preface, as well as to philosophy of language more generally. Grice himself did not use the terms 'semantic content', 'semantic contribution', or 'proposition expressed', terms that have been very important to our discussion thus far. Instead, Grice employed a notion very close in key ways to that of semantic content, for which his term was 'what is said'. For Grice, what is said is in large part determined by conventional meaning (in combination with contextual factors to arrive at, for example, referents for indexicals). One necessary condition for a sentence S to say that p, according to Grice, is that 'S means "p" in virtue of the particular meanings of the elements of S, their order, and their syntactical character'.[8] (Grice 1989: 81.) For Grice, whether a sentence is true or false is a matter of whether *what the sentence says* is true or false. In the current section, on Grice's theory, I employ Grice's terminology.

Grice developed his theory of implicature in part as a way of accounting for some problematic intuitions about the English equivalents of logical vocabulary, like 'and'. According to the traditional understanding of 'and', *p and q* will be true just in the case that p is true and q is true. But in everyday use, a claim of the form *p and q* often seems to mean much more than this—it often carries, for example, a suggestion of temporal order, as in (7) below.

(7) They got married and had children.

(7) seems to mean that the marriage took place before the children were born, and it would generally be judged false if the children preceded

---

[7] The 'nearly' here is important: In Chapter 5 and Appendix A, I will discuss two exceptions to this. The first, Scott Soames's (2002) view, stays close in spirit to the ones discussed here. The second, David Braun's (1998) view, deviates in important ways from the standard strategies under discussion here. It is also worth noting that Salmon and Soames do not fully commit themselves to the idea that Gricean conversational implicatures should be invoked to explain recalcitrant intuitions. It is, however, the only detailed approach they discuss.

[8] Grice also holds that an utterance cannot say that p unless the speaker means that p. This part of his view is often (perhaps justly) neglected.

the marriage. Grice argued, however, that these judgments are mistaken—what (7) says is just what the traditional logical understanding of 'and' would dictate. Nonetheless, utterances of (7) may often convey more than this. They do this, Grice suggested, via a mechanism he called 'conversational implicature'. Grice argued that often our truth conditional intuitions reflect not what is said by an utterance but what is conversationally implicated. That is why it may seem to us (wrongly) that an utterance of a sentence like (7) is false if the marriage took place after the children were born.

Grice suggests that conversation, as a cooperative endeavour, is governed by certain principles of cooperation, close relatives of which he takes to govern other cooperative pursuits as well. More specifically, he proposes that conversation is governed by an overarching Cooperative Principle and four maxims of cooperation.

- *Cooperative Principle:* 'Make your contribution such as is required, at the stage at which it occurs, by the accepted purpose or direction of the talk exchange in which you are engaged' (Grice 1989: 26).
- *Maxim of Quantity:* 'Make your contribution as informative as is required (for the current purposes of the exchange)...Do not make your contribution more informative than is required' (Grice 1989: 26).
- *Maxim of Quality:* 'Try to make your contribution one that is true' (Grice 1989: 21).
- *Maxim of Relation:* 'Be relevant' (Grice 1989: 21).
- *Maxim of Manner:* 'Be perspicuous' (Grice 1989: 21). This maxim includes, among others, the submaxim 'be orderly'.

Grice does not think that all people adhere to the Cooperative Principle and its maxims at all times. Nor does he think that we ever consciously reflect on this principle. Rather, his idea is that we all tacitly presume each other to be following the Cooperative Principle unless we have reason to suppose otherwise. In order to maintain this presumption that others are being cooperative, we will make supplementary assumptions. This tendency of audiences, and speakers' knowledge of this tendency, are important to making possible communication via conversational implicature.

Grice suggests that all this is what brings it about that an utterance of (7) carries a suggestion of temporal order: the audience can reasonably assume that the speaker is following the Maxim of Manner and therefore presenting events in the order in which they occurred. Since the marriage is mentioned before the children, then, the audience will assume that the marriage came first. This assumption—that the marriage preceded the children—is a conversational implicature. Grice does not take the audience to always go through such reasoning consciously, or even at all. They may instead leap directly to the implicature. Instead, his point is that this reasoning is available. Its availability makes it the case that audiences might be reasonable to read in extra information. Grice's story about how implicatures are generated also serves to illustrate how speakers might systematically make use of audiences' assumptions in order to convey more than they, strictly speaking, say. The possibility of such reasoning on the audience's part—the *calculability* of conversational implicatures—is one requirement for their existence: any putative conversational implicature must be calculable.

Grice also gives a more formal characterisation of conversational implicature. According to Grice, a person conversationally implicates that q by saying that p only if[9]:

(1) he is to be presumed to be following the conversational maxims, or at least the Cooperative Principle;
(2) the supposition that he is aware that, or thinks that, q is required to make his saying. . . p (or doing so in *those* terms) consistent with this presumption;[10] and
(3) the speaker thinks (and would expect the hearer to think that the speaker thinks) that it is within the competence of the hearer to work out, or grasp intuitively, that the supposition mentioned in (2) is required. (Grice 1989: 30-1)

---

[9] Grice introduces these conditions as follows: 'A man who, by (in, when) saying (or making as if to say) that p has implicated that q, may be said to have conversationally implicated that q, provided that. . . ' (1989: 30). It is standard for logicians to translate 'provided that' as 'if', and therefore to view it as presenting merely sufficient conditions. It is clear, however, that this is not how Grice is using 'provided that'. On pages 39–40, he draws on these conditions in order to work out some additional features that conversational implicatures *must* have (such as cancelability). His use of these conditions makes it clear that he takes them to be necessary ones. And Grice is not alone in this usage of 'provided that'. It is well-known that 'provided that' is commonly used roughly in accord with 'if and only if'—as a means of introducing necessary and sufficient conditions. It is fairly standard to interpret Grice as providing necessary and sufficient conditions for conversational implicature (e.g. Davis 1998: 13; Levinson 2000: 15). However, Grice is only concerned with conditions that must be met *by those who have implicated that q*, and implicating that q may have its own necessary conditions. As a result, I hesitate to assume that the conditions following 'provided that' are *both* necessary and sufficient for conversational implicature. For that reason, I have interpreted Grice above as using 'provided that' to introduce necessary conditions for conversational implicature. In fact, it would make no difference to my arguments if the conditions were taken to be both necessary and sufficient.

[10] In clause 2, I have suppressed Grice's reference to *making as if to say*, which is not relevant to the present discussion.

Clause (2) of this characterisation fits well with the emphasis we have already seen on calculability. If an implicature cannot be worked out by the audience, it is not calculable. Grice writes,

The presence of a conversational implicature must be capable of being worked out. . . To work out that a particular conversational implicature is present, the hearer will rely on the following data: (1) the conventional meaning of the words used, together with the identity of any references that may be involved; (2) the Cooperative Principle and its maxims; (3) the context, linguistic or otherwise, of the utterance; (4) other items of background knowledge; and (5) the fact (or supposed fact) that all relevant items falling under the previous headings are available to both participants and both participants know or assume this to be the case. A general pattern for the working out of a conversational implicature might be given as follows: 'He has said that p; there is no reason to suppose that he is not observing the maxims, or at least the Cooperative Principle; he could not be doing this unless he thought that q; he knows (and knows that I know he knows) that I can see that the supposition that he thinks that q is required; he has done nothing to stop me thinking that q; he intends me to think, or at least is willing to allow me to think, that q; and so he has implicated that q'. (Grice 1989: 31)

Grice notes that several features of conversational implicatures can be predicted from this discussion. One is that they will vary with context: In some contexts, a presumption of cooperativeness may be present that is not present in others. Conversational implicatures cannot be generated unless the presumption of cooperativeness is in force, so a sentence whose utterance generates an implicature in one context may fail to do so in another. But contextual variation may arise in other ways as well. Audiences are meant to rely on background assumptions that help in guiding them to the speaker's intended message. In different contexts, different background assumptions will come into play. As a result, utterances of one sentence in two different contexts may carry two different implicatures.

Grice also predicts that conversational implicatures will be *cancelable*. Because contexts vary in the ways described above, one may cancel an implicature that would otherwise be present by making it clear that the audience should not make particular assumptions—because maxims are being violated, or certain background assumptions are false. For example, one who utters (7C) is pointing out that the maxim of manner is not being followed.

(7C) They got married and had children, but not in that order.

As a result, the audience will not assume that the marriage happened before the children. The manner-derived implicature that the marriage preceded the children will therefore not be present. This cancelability counts against the rival theory that (7) *says* something like (7T).[11]

(7) They got married and had children.
(7T) They got married and *then* had children.

If (7) said the same thing as (7T), then, the argument goes, (7C) would make about as much sense as (7TC).

(7TC) They got married and *then* had children, but not necessarily in that order.

(7TC), which attempts to cancel a claim that is a part of what is said, is incoherent; but (7C) is not. The fact that the suggestion of temporal order in (7C) is cancelable, then, serves as evidence that it is not a part of what (7) says—and as evidence that it is a conversational implicature.

Grice does not offer any hard and fast rules for determining whether some suggestion carried by an utterance is a conversational implicature or a part of what is said. He does, however, suggest that traits like cancelability and calculability can serve as a defeasible guide: if some putative conversational implicature turns out not to be cancelable or calculable, it is not a conversational implicature; the presence of cancelability or calculability are evidence in favour of conversational implicature, but they do not guarantee it.[12]

1.1.2.2 Belief reporting, Naïve Millians, and implicature

Naïve Millians argue that our anti-substitution intuitions do not really reflect the truth conditions of attitude reporting utterances; instead, they reflect something else. Traditionally, the 'something else' has been taken to be conversational implicatures (Salmon 1986)—although

---

[11] It counts strongly against the claim that *all* utterances of (7) express something like (7T)—and this sort of view was what Grice was concerned to refute. However, it is far from decisive evidence against the claim that *some* utterances of (7) may express something like (7T). For example, one might suppose that (7) is ambiguous between two readings, one that carries a suggestion that the marriage preceded the children, and another which doesn't. A defender of such a view could argue that (7C) is an instance of disambiguation, rather than one of cancellation of an implicature. For good discussions of this move's availability, see Crimmins 1992: 21–2; Sadock 1978: 293–4.

[12] Grice also discusses other traits of conversational implicatures, such as non-detachability and not being relevant to truth conditions. But it is difficult to arrive at a non-question-begging way to use these even as defeasible tests. See Sadock (1978).

Naïve Millians do not commit themselves decisively on this point.[13] A key piece of evidence in favour of this view has been the contextual variability and cancelability of our anti-substitution intuitions. This evidence helps to support an implicature view in two separate ways: first, it counts against alternative views that cannot accommodate these features; and second, it provides defeasible support for the idea that the intuitions are due to conversational implicatures.

It is fairly easy to find cases that show contextual variation in our truth-conditional intuitions about belief-reporting sentences, and in our intuitions about substitution inferences involving these sentences. Suppose I am discussing what people in general think of Bob Dylan's singing abilities, and the person I'm talking to knows him only as 'Bob Dylan'. I've been told (truthfully) that Glenda, a childhood friend, who knows him only as 'Robert Zimmerman', believes that he has a beautiful voice. Specifically, someone I trust has uttered sentence (8):

(8) Glenda believes that Robert Zimmerman has a beautiful voice.

I may report this with (8*):

(8*) Glenda believes that Bob Dylan has a beautiful voice.

(8*) seems true, even though Glenda would never assent to it. To know that (8*) is true, moreover, we don't need to know anything at all about how Glenda thinks of her childhood friend Robert Zimmerman. All that matters is his identity, and the fact that she liked his voice. This suggests that substitution inferences are sometimes perfectly acceptable. Cases like this are problematic for theories committed to the claim that substitution of co-referential names is never guaranteed to preserve truth in belief reports. Moreover, an utterance of the very same sentence in an alternative conversational context may take a different truth value. Suppose now that Glenda is participating in a marketing poll which asks for her opinions of various singers' voices. One of the names on the list is 'Bob Dylan'. I'm asked to predict her responses. If I replied with sentence (8*), intuition has it, my utterance would be false. There is, then, an important element of contextual variation in our intuitions about substitution. And this contextual variation fits well with an explanation in terms of conversational implicature.

---

[13] As noted in footnote 7, some recent Millian work—like Soames (2002) and Braun (1998)—makes use of alternatives to implicature.

It is also pretty easy to find cases that look like ones of implicature cancellation. Consider again the conversation about the marketing poll. Now suppose that I utter (8C) in reply to a request to predict Glenda's responses:

(8C) Glenda believes that Bob Dylan has a beautiful voice, but she wouldn't say so using the name 'Bob Dylan'.

My utterance of (8C) does not seem false, or even misleading. If I answered the question with (8), I would convey that Glenda holds the belief in question under the name 'Bob Dylan'. But if I answered with (8C), this would no longer be conveyed. This looks very much like the cancellation of an implicature.

1.1.2.3 A Naïve Implicature view[14]

With this support in hand, proponents of Naïve implicature theory have argued that a view like theirs can accommodate our intuitions better than views that simply block substitution of co-referential names in attitude reports. Nathan Salmon's (1986, 1989)[15] Naïve implicature view is the best-developed one, so I will focus on it. On this view, a name's sole semantic content, in any sort of sentence, is its referent. A belief report is true just in case the believer stands in the relation of believing to the singular proposition expressed by the sentence in the embedded clause of the belief report. (This proposition is a structured Russellian proposition, made up of individuals and properties.) The relation of believing is the existential generalisation of a 3-place relation, BEL, which involves a believer, a proposition, and a guise under which that proposition is apprehended (guises are something like sentences). The BEL relation holds iff the believer is disposed to inwardly assent to the proposition under the guise. Since belief is the existential generalisation of the BEL relation, a believer believes a proposition iff she is disposed to assent to it under *some* guise.[16] Thus, the particular guise under which a proposition is believed has no bearing on the truth conditions of a belief ascription, and substitution of co-referential names always preserves truth conditions.

---

[14] Some material in this section is taken from Saul (1998), with kind permission of Springer publishing.

[15] Salmon does not fully commit himself to conversational implicature as his explanation for anti-substitution intuitions. However, it is the only mechanism that he discusses in any detail.

[16] This particular version is from Salmon (1986: 111).

Salmon argues that, while utterances of (9) must express exactly the same proposition as utterances of (9*), they will generally pragmatically convey different information.

(9) Lois believes that Superman flies.
(9*) Lois believes that Clark flies.

An utterance of (9) will implicate something like the information expressed by (9G), and an utterance of (9*) will implicate something like the information expressed by (9*G).

(9G) Lois believes that Superman flies under a guise like 'Superman can fly'.
(9*G) Lois believes that Clark flies under a guise like 'Clark can fly'.

Speakers are often unaware of the difference between semantically expressed and pragmatically conveyed information. As a result, their truth-conditional intuitions—which *should* tell us about what is expressed—instead often reflect what is implicated. So a speaker's intuitions about an utterance of (9) may reflect their verdict regarding its implicature—something more like (9G); and similarly for (9*) and (9*G). It is obvious that (9*G) may diverge in truth value from (9G), so they wrongly think that (9) and (9*) may diverge in truth value.

The same sort of explanation is used to deal with negative belief reports. We would be inclined to say that (10) is true along with (9):

(10) Lois doesn't believe that Clark flies.

According to Salmon, however, if (9) is true then (10) is not true: If Lois believes that Superman can fly, then she believes that Clark can fly—so it can't be true that she doesn't believe that Clark can fly. The belief relation holds between a believer, B, and a proposition, p, whenever B is disposed to assent to p under any guise at all. In order to count as not believing p, then, there must be no guise under which B is disposed to assent to p. This is clearly not the case: Lois believes that Clark can fly, under the guise 'Superman flies'.

However, Salmon also defines the notion of *withholding belief*. A believer B *withholds belief* from a proposition p iff there is *some* guise under which B grasps p but is not disposed to assent to it. In order to count as withholding belief from p, then, all that is needed is *some* guise under which B grasps but is not disposed to assent to p. And Lois does indeed withhold belief from the proposition that Clark can fly, because she is not disposed to assent to it under the guise 'Clark can fly'.

Salmon suggests that when we utter (10) we are trying to convey something about withholding belief. Specifically, we are trying to convey that there is some guise, that Lois understands, under which she *is not disposed to assent to* the proposition in question. If there is such a guise, it is true that Lois withholds belief from the proposition that Superman can fly. According to this story, something like (10G) is implicated by (10).

(10G) Lois withholds belief from the proposition that Clark can fly.

Salmon maintains that our intuitions about (10) derive from focusing not on what (10) says but on what it implicates—something akin to (10G). The reason we might think that (10) is true is that we mistake *not believing* for *withholding belief.* (10G), unlike (10), may be true even if (9) is true.

The story, as described above, is short on details. Among the things we should want to know are (i) exactly what the implicated propositions are—that they are *something like* (9G), (9*G), and (10G) is surely not enough; (ii) what maxims are involved in generating the implicature, and (iii) how is the implicature calculated? There have been attempts made to answer these questions, but none of them have been entirely satisfying.[17]

Naïve implicature theory has not, it is fair to say, convinced everyone. Some objections turn on the nature of conversational implicature. For example: Francois Recanati (1993: 325–41) insists that—in order to accord with Grice's calculability requirement—what is said and what is implicated must be psychologically accessible in a way that they would not be on Salmon's account. Mitch Green calls attention to certain differences between the hypothesised belief reporting implicatures and the sorts of implicatures likely to generate confusion of the sort required for Salmon's explanation (Green 1998). Stephen Schiffer raises concerns about the mechanics of implicature calculation (Schiffer 1987; Salmon 1989). But the strongest objection to Naïve implicature theory remains the most obvious: it violates our truth-conditional intuitions about attitude reports. Sophisticated objectors will accept that sometimes we must, and should, settle for an account that violates our intuitions, as long as it is accompanied by an explanation of these violations. They do not, however, accept that this is the situation with respect to attitude reporting. Instead, they maintain that we must find an account that agrees with our anti-substitution intuitions, and that we should refuse to accept one that does not.

---

[17] For discussion of these accounts, and problems with them, see Braun (1998); Saul (1998).

1.1.3 Belief reporting and contextualist theories

For some time, Naïve implicature theorists had a strong response to the line of argument above: although their theory violated *anti*-substitution intuitions, their opponents' theories violated *pro*-substitution intuitions (see e.g. Soames 1988). After all, we have just seen a clear example of substitution *success*. In the context of our conversation about Bob Dylan's singing abilities, (8*) seems true simply because (8) is true—we don't need to know anything about how Glenda thinks of Dylan/Zimmerman to make the inference to (8*).

(8) Glenda believes that Robert Zimmerman has a beautiful voice.
(8*) Glenda believes that Bob Dylan has a beautiful voice.

On a Fregean theory, this inference is never acceptable, as 'Robert Zimmerman' and 'Bob Dylan' simply have different senses. Such a theory, then, violates our intuitions of substitution success. Naïve implicature theorists, however, uphold these intuitions. In addition their theory *predicts* that intuitions about substitution will vary with context—a puzzling fact for the traditional Fregean. Naïve Millianism, then, was in a position to explain far more of our intuitions than Fregeanism (even if some of these explanations were less than fully satisfying).

But this happy situation for the Naïve Millian did not last long. There are now a variety of theories on the market that purport to accommodate contextual variation in our intuitions just as well as Naïve implicature theory can. Moreover, these theories aim to accommodate our intuitions by *agreeing* with them—*all* of them—rather than explaining them away. These theories are contextualist ones, according to which what is expressed by a belief report—and so, its truth conditions—may vary with context. As a result, the acceptability of substitution inferences also varies with context. Theories like these offer the hope of accommodating *all* our substitution-related intuitions, those in favour and those against. I will examine two of these theories, those offered by Mark Crimmins (Crimmins and Perry 1989; Mark Richard 1990; and Crimmins 1992).[18]

---

[18] These are not the only contextualist theories on the market. For example, Graeme Forbes's neo-Fregean theory (1990, 1993) is a contextualist one. (Forbes's view was not contextualist in its initial formulation. However, Forbes included contextualist elements in his 1993, largely in response to criticisms from Crimmins (1993) and Richard (1993).) Although I do not discuss Forbes's theory of beliefil reporting here, I discuss his theory of simple sentences in the next chapter.

1.1.3.1 Crimmins

Crimmins (Crimmins and Perry 1989; Crimmins 1992) holds that the sole contribution of a name to the proposition expressed by a sentence containing it is its referent. Crimmins, like Salmon and Soames, holds that propositions are structured, and made up of individuals and properties. For Crimmins, non-belief reporting sentences that differ only in the presence of different co-referential names express the same proposition. Further, the embedded sentence in a belief report expresses just the same proposition as it would if not embedded. Nonetheless, Crimmins does not hold that substitution of co-referential names must always preserve truth conditions. Crimmins maintains that the truth value of a belief report does not depend just on whether its subject has a belief with the specified content.

There are a number of things that are sometimes meant by 'belief'. On one understanding, beliefs are individuated by propositional content: two people may have the same belief because they are in mental states of the same sort with the same content. On another understanding, beliefs are particular mental states—two people cannot share the same belief, although they may have beliefs with the same content. Crimmins holds that the semantic content of a belief report informs us about both the propositional contents of beliefs and the particular mental states that bear these contents. Substitution of co-referential names is not licensed on Crimmins's view, because a true belief report specifies the belief—the particular mental state—whose content is the proposition expressed by the embedded clause. This belief is itself structured in much the same way as the proposition that is its content. Where the proposition contains individuals and properties, the belief contains *notions* and *ideas*, their private, representational counterparts. It is by specifying notions and ideas that, according to Crimmins, a belief report specifies not just *what* proposition is believed, but how that proposition is believed.

Notions and ideas are specified by contextually-supplied, unarticulated constituents of the proposition expressed by a belief report. (An unarticulated constituent—as the concept is used here—is simply a propositional constituent that is not represented by any linguistic unit in the sentence that expresses the proposition (Crimmins 1992: 16)). A belief report is true just in case the believer has a belief with the specified propositional content that involves the contextually-specified notions and ideas in the right way. The specification of notions and ideas amounts to a specification of the relevant belief whose content is that proposition. Very roughly, the truth conditions of belief reports can be given as follows:

An utterance *u* of a belief report, *A believes that S*, is true iff *A* has some belief whose content is the proposition expressed by *S*, and this belief involves the notions specified in the right way.

Because which notions and ideas are specified will vary with context, the truth value of a belief reporting sentence may vary with context. In the discussion of the marketing poll, my utterance of (8*) will require a very specific sort of notion for its truth.

(8*) Glenda believes that Bob Dylan has a beautiful voice.

The report will only be made true by a belief of Glenda's with the specified content *that involves a notion she associates with the name 'Bob Dylan'*. The notion that Glenda associates with 'Robert Zimmerman' does not meet this condition, so even though she has a belief with the requisite content (that Bob Dylan has a beautiful voice), my report is still false. But when I utter (8*) in the discussion of Dylan's singing abilities, the requirements will be quite loose—so loose that a belief involving the notion Glenda associates with 'Robert Zimmerman' *will* make the report true. Crimmins's account, then, holds out the promise of agreeing with *all* our intuitions about substitution—both in favour and opposed. And this is a promise that neither Naïve Millians nor traditional Fregeans can make.

1.1.3.2 Richard

Richard's account makes use of proposition-like entities that he calls RAMs. Every sentence expresses a RAM, which is a fusion of that sentence and its 'Russellian interpretation' (Richard 1990: 131)—what Naïve Millians would take to be the proposition it expresses.[19] This Russellian interpretation is a structured proposition consisting of individuals and properties, with the contribution of a name being solely its referent. Every believer has a representational system (RS) that consists of RAMs that she accepts. A belief report is true in a context just in case there is some RAM in the believer's RS that is an acceptable translation (in that context) of the RAM in the report's content clause. What counts

---

[19] Richard, like other theorists including David Braun (2000: 203), uses 'Russellianism' to refer to the view I have called 'Naïve Millianism'.

as an acceptable translation is determined by the intentions and interests of the speaker and audience. As a result of this variation in acceptable translations, the truth conditions of belief reporting sentences will vary with context.

A little loosely, and in more familiar terms, the idea is this: What a sentence expresses is a matter of both the sentence and what is normally called its propositional content. A belief report is true if the believer (a) has a belief with the propositional content specified by the report; and (b) the believer holds this belief under a sentence that counts as an appropriate translation of the one in the report's 'that'-clause. What counts as appropriate will vary with context, so the truth value of a belief report will vary with context.

To see how this works, consider again my two utterances of (8*).

(8*) Glenda believes that Bob Dylan has a beautiful voice.

When discussing the marketing poll, there will be quite a tight restriction on translation in force: the content clause in (8*) will not count as an acceptable translation of the content clause in (8).

(8) Glenda believes that Robert Zimmerman has a beautiful voice.

As a result, my utterance of (8*) will be false. But when discussing people's opinions of Dylan's singing abilities, standards of translation are looser—we don't care whether or not Glenda would accept the sentence 'Bob Dylan has a beautiful voice'. In this context, then, (8*) will be true. Like Crimmins's account, then, Richard's seems able to accommodate both pro- and anti-substitution intuitions.

Contextual variation accounts like Crimmins's and Richard's have a great deal in their favour. Because they allow for contextual variation in the truth values of belief reports, they hold out the promise of agreeing with all of our substitution-related intuitions. According to these accounts, the reason it seems to us that substitution fails in many belief reporting utterances yet succeeds in others is that *it does*. This is, obviously, a very desirable result. Moreover, even the promise of such a result is an appealing one. Once we see its possibility, it is very hard to accept an account like Salmon and Soames's that rules this out. For this reason, belief reporting accounts that allow for contextual variation in the semantics of belief reports remain appealing despite objections that have been raised to the specific accounts on the market.[20]

[20] For some of these objections, see Sider (1995), Soames (1995), and Saul (1992, 1999*a, b*)

1.2 SIMPLE SENTENCES AND SUBSTITUTION

Simple sentences in which substitution seems to fail demand modifications to this picture of the debate. We can see the difficulty that they pose initially as a dilemma for those who oppose Naïve Millianism—that is, nearly all philosophers of language. For these theorists, the most unacceptable consequence of Naïve Millianism is generally taken to be its disagreement with anti-substitution intuitions about belief reports. A theory that fails to accord with anti-substitution intuitions, they insist, should be rejected. Instead, we should prefer a theory that respects these intuitions by blocking substitution in belief reports.

Any theory that attempts to block substitution only in belief reports (or other special substitution-resistant contexts) will fail to block substitution in simple sentences—those that do not contain any propositional attitude reporting constructions (or any other constructions traditionally associated with substitution failure). This is traditionally thought to be an acceptable—indeed, desirable—feature. But now imagine that (11) is an accurate description of the events on a Metropolis street. (11*), which we get from substituting co-referential names, seems false.

(11) Clark Kent went into the phone booth and Superman came out.
(11*) Superman went into the phone booth and Clark Kent came out.

We get similar failures of substitution in sentences like the following:

(12) Clark Kent always arrived at the scene just after one of Superman's daring rescues.
(12*) Superman always arrived at the scene just after one of Clark Kent's daring rescues.
(13) Hesperus appears in the evening and Phosphorus appears in the morning.
(13*) Hesperus appears in the evening and Hesperus appears in the morning.

Relatedly, (14) seems like it might be true, even though (14*) is surely false.

(14) Superman leaps more tall buildings than Clark Kent does.
(14*) Superman leaps more tall buildings than Superman does.

Such sentence pairs are not confined to the world of fiction, and people really do utter them. In fact, (15) and (16) come from *The NY Review of Books* and *World Traveller* magazine, respectively:

(15) Shostakovich always signalled his connections to the classical traditions of St Petersburg, even if he was forced to live in Leningrad.[21]

(15*) Shostakovich always signalled his connections the classical traditions of Leningrad, even if he was forced to live in St Petersburg.

(16) So in some ways, we've made a dual biography of Mark Twain and Sam Clemens.[22]

(16*) So in some ways, we've made a dual biography of Mark Twain and Mark Twain.

Intuitively, substitution fails in the pairs of sentences above. As we will see, this poses problems for all the theories we have discussed so far. Yet there is reason to believe that it poses a special problem for those who oppose Naïve Millianism.

1.2.1 A challenge to opponents of Naïve Millianism

A proponent of a theory opposed to Naïve Millianism is, seemingly, faced with a choice:[23]

- Option 1: Extend the theory so that it blocks substitution in simple sentences as well as in sentences containing standard substitution-blocking constructions.

- Option 2: Maintain that our anti-substitution intuitions about simple sentences are in error. On this option, the opponent of Naïve Millianism must explain away anti-substitution intuitions about simple sentences while insisting that it is unacceptable for the Naïve Millian to explain away anti-substitution intuitions about belief reports. She will, then, need to offer a very good reason to suppose that anti-substitution intuitions about belief reports demand a kind of respect that those about simple sentences do not.

Simple sentences, then, present a challenge to those who oppose Naïve Millianism. If they wish to insist that respect for anti-substitution intuitions demands an account that accords with these intuitions, they must offer a semantics that accords with anti-substitution intuitions about simple sentences. If they cannot do this, one of the strongest objections to Naïve Millianism—that it violates anti-substitution intuitions—is

---

[21] *NY Review of Books* (2004), 10 June: 14.

[22] Ken Burns, quoted in Ammeson (2002: 40).

[23] The 'seemingly' is important. In what is to come, we will explore other options, including that of denying that the names in question are co-referential (Pitt 2001), which is discussed in Chapter 2.

substantially weakened. If *every theory* is doomed to violate anti-substitution intuitions, it is no longer so devastating to point out that Naïve Millianism does so.

The first strategy has proved more popular than I expected it to be when I initially posed this dilemma.[24] In the next chapter, I will explore the substitution-blocking proposals for simple sentences that have appeared in the literature. Here, however, I want only to show why it is that standard accounts of belief reporting cannot be straightforwardly extended to block substitution in simple sentences.

1.2.2 Why standard accounts cannot easily adapt

Standard accounts cannot be easily adapted to block substitution in simple sentences. To see this, we will look at two sorts of account: a traditional Fregean one, and the contextualist accounts noted earlier. Our examination will not conclusively prove that these accounts cannot be adapted to cover simple sentence cases. But it will help to indicate the difficulty of carrying out such an adaptation.

1.2.2.1 Fregean theories

Traditionally, Fregean theories rely on senses to block substitution. In ordinary contexts, terms refer to their references, while in (the embedded clauses of) belief reports they refer to their customary senses. The reason (9) and (9*) may differ in truth value is that different senses are referred to by the terms 'Superman' and 'Clark Kent' within the belief clauses.

(9) Lois believes that Superman flies.
(9*) Lois believes that Clark Kent flies.

On the other hand, (17) and (17*) cannot differ in truth value:

(17) Superman flies.
(17*) Clark Kent flies.

---

[24] Actually, this is a slightly more general form of the dilemma I originally posed in Saul (1997*a*). There, the second option was somewhat different: I claimed that those who oppose naïve implicature theory would presumably explain away anti-substitution intuitions about simple sentences as due to implicatures. As I have become more aware of the possibilities (and, indeed, need) for non-implicature-based explanations of mistaken anti-substitution intuitions (about both simple sentences and others), I have decided the problem should now be posed in this more general way.

In the absence of an opacity-inducing construction, the terms 'Superman' and 'Clark Kent' refer to their customary referents. These are the same, so the two sentences cannot differ in truth value. Substitution may only be blocked if there is an opacity-producing construction that can bring about a reference shift. Simple sentences in which substitution seems to fail, then, pose obvious problems: they are cases in which there are substitution failures despite the lack of constructions to bring about a reference shift. On a traditional Fregean view, this is impossible, as the names in such sentences must refer to their customary references, thus guaranteeing that substitution of co-referential names will preserve truth value.

Nonetheless, one might think that Fregean theories could adapt by allowing reference shifts to *sometimes* take place even in the absence of the standard opacity-inducing constructions. Such a view, then, introduces a sort of context-dependence into a Fregean semantics. On this view, names in simple sentences would sometimes refer to their customary references and sometimes to their customary senses. There would be many technical niceties to be worked out—deciding, for example, when a name refers to its customary sense and when it refers to its customary reference. But assume for the sake of the discussion that a satisfactory answer could be given. Even if this problem and others of its ilk could be solved, it seems to me that a straightforward adaptation of a Fregean theory is unlikely to succeed. The reason for this is that senses just do not seem like the sorts of things that names could plausibly be referring to in simple sentences. Consider, for example, sentence (11):

(11) Clark Kent went into the phone booth and Superman came out.

This sentence can only be true if the thing referred to by 'Clark Kent' went into the phone booth and the thing referred to by 'Superman' came out. But if that thing is a sense, this just isn't possible: Senses do not go into and out of phone booths. Allowing names to refer to their senses in simple sentences like those discussed here would yield nonsense, rather than intuitively correct truth values.

It is important to note, however, that there are some simple sentence intuitions that are straightforwardly explicable on Fregean theories: those of people who do not realise that the names involved co-refer. To see this, assume that Lois is unaware that 'Superman' and 'Clark Kent' co-refer. Assume further that Lois takes (17) and (17*) to differ in truth value. This anti-substitution intuition of Lois's should come as no surprise to the Fregean. After all, the Fregean takes (17) and (17*) to express different propositions. Even though these propositions must in fact take the same truth value, it is perfectly understandable that someone like Lois—unaware of the relevant facts—will take them to differ in truth value.[25]

The problem posed by simple sentences, then, is not one concerning the intuitions of those unaware of the relevant double lives—those Joseph Moore (1999) has called *the unenlightened*. The problem posed by simple sentences is that it is not only the unenlightened who think sentences like (11) and (11*) may differ in truth value. We (many of us, anyway) think this as well, and we are enlightened.[26] This fact—the fact that even when we know all the relevant facts (11) and (11*) may seem like they may differ in truth value—is what poses difficulties for Fregean theories.

It is important to observe that a parallel point holds for belief reporting sentences. If Fregeans were only trying to explain the anti-substitution intuitions of the unenlightened, there would be no need for the doctrine of reference shift. The fact that (9) and (9*) express different propositions provides a sufficient explanation for the anti-substitution intuitions of those unaware of the relevant facts.

(9) Lois believes that Superman flies.
(9*) Lois believes that Clark Kent flies

The doctrine of reference shift is needed because anti-substitution intuitions about belief reporting sentences are not confined to the unenlightened. We have the intuition that substitution fails, and we are enlightened. Even when apprised of the relevant facts, most people still think that (9) and (9*) differ in truth value. The desire to vindicate *these* intuitions—which can't be explained as deriving from ignorance of the relevant facts—is what motivates the doctrine of reference shift.

Fregean theories, then, cannot readily be adapted to accommodate anti-substitution intuitions about simple sentences. Although they can easily explain the intuitions of those unaware of relevant facts, this is

---

[25] Alex Barber (2000) also makes this point.
[26] It is worth acknowledging at the outset that although many of the enlightened have these intuitions, and seem to have them quite strongly, not all of the enlightened seem to have them (or, at least, they do not have them very strongly). While this is an important point, I am setting it aside for now to focus on the problem of explaining the intuitions of the enlightened who *do* have anti-substitution intuitions about simple sentences. These intuitions will be my primary focus until I reach Chapter 6. In Chapter 6, I will explore variation in intuitions and in strength of intuitions, and I will address the issue of enlightened people who lack anti-substitution intuitions about simple sentences.

beside the point. In order to respect anti-substitution intuitions about simple sentences as they respect those about belief reporting sentences, Fregeans need to accommodate not just these intuitions but also those of the enlightened—those fully aware of all the relevant double lives.[27]

1.2.2.2 Contextual variation theories

As we saw earlier, some of the most promising recent approaches to propositional attitude reporting have crucially involved context-dependent elements in the semantics of such reports. It is natural to wonder how such accounts might fare at accommodating intuitions about simple sentences.

1.2.2.2.1 Richard's account

We have seen that on Mark Richard's (1990) account, a belief report is true just in case the sentence in its content clause serves as an acceptable translation of a sentence that the believer accepts. Standards for acceptable translation vary with context. Substitution of co-referential terms, then, fails if there are no acceptable translations mapping the sentence in the report's context clause to one that the believer accepts.

Other propositional attitudes are dealt with in a parallel manner. For example: An utterance of *A doubts that S* will be true just in case (roughly) *S* serves as an acceptable translation of some sentence whose truth *A* doubts. It is less easy, however, to see how to extend this account beyond the realm of attitude attribution. With a belief report, it makes sense to raise the issue of whether a particular sentence is an acceptable translation of one of the believer's beliefs, and similarly for reports of doubts. But what could possibly be the analogous issue with simple sentences? Nobody's psychological states are being reported by such sentences, after all. We cannot even begin to see whose translations of the uttered sentence would be relevant, or how such translations might affect truth conditions: does the speaker need to accept them? The audience? Someone else?

1.2.2.2.2 Crimmins's account

According to Crimmins's account, belief reports specify not just the content of the belief being reported, but something more—some details of how the belief is held. They do this by specifying the notions and

---

[27] For convenience, I sometimes use the term 'double lives' as a kind of shorthand. Planets and cities, of course, don't lead lives, let alone double lives.

ideas—concrete psychological particulars—involved in the reported belief. Which notions and ideas get described will vary with context, and this is what determines whether substitution fails or succeeds. It is straightforward to adapt this account to cover propositional attitudes other than believing. It is far from obvious, though, how this could be made to work for simple sentences. These sentences do not involve agents whose mental states are under discussion, so it is difficult to see whose notions and ideas might be at stake in simple sentences. Even if one could find an answer to this worry, however, other worries would remain. Notions and ideas—concrete mental particulars—*might* go in and out of phone booths, but only because those whose concrete mental particulars they are go in and out of phone booths. Recourse to these entities does not seem likely to help with sentences that do not ascribe psychological states.

1.2.2.2.3 What these accounts can do

Despite these difficulties, it is important to note that these accounts—like Fregean ones—can handle *some* simple sentence intuitions. In particular, they are perfectly adequate for explaining the intuitions of the unenlightened.

Consider again (11) and (11*).

(11) Clark Kent went into the phone booth and Superman came out.
(11*) Superman went into the phone booth and Clark Kent came out.

If we focus only on the unenlightened, our task is that of explaining why it is that one who doesn't realise 'Clark Kent' and 'Superman' co-refer might think that (11) is true while (11*) is false.

Mark Richard, like the Fregean, takes (11) and (11*) to express different propositions (or, in his terminology, RAMs), simply because they are different sentences. It is easy to explain, then, why someone *un*aware of Clark Kent's double life might take the sentences to differ in truth value. These sentences, for Richard, simply say different things. One who is unaware that 'Clark Kent' and 'Superman' co-refer is in no position to realise that these different sentences, which say different things, must take the same truth value. Such a person's intuitions are easy to explain: utterances of (11) and (11*) express different propositions; an unenlightened person who understands these sentences will have no reason to suppose that they must take the same truth value; so such a person may well assign different truth values to (11) and (11*).

Mark Crimmins, unlike Mark Richard, would say that (11) and (11*) express the same proposition. However, his account makes much of the fact that more than one belief (in the sense of psychological state) might have this proposition as its content. As long as one associates different notions with 'Clark Kent' and 'Superman' (as an unenlightened person would), one might well read and assent to (11) while insisting that (11*) is false—simply because one represents the proposition expressed by (11) and (11*) different ways.

However, neither of these responses is sufficient as an answer to the problem posed by simple sentences. The intuitions of the unenlightened can be dismissed as resulting from false beliefs. They think (11) and (11*) can differ in truth value, but they're *wrong*. And we know why they're wrong—they simply don't realise that 'Superman' and 'Clark Kent' name the same individual. But enlightened intuitions cannot be dismissed so easily. Enlightened people like us also think that (11) and (11*) can differ in truth value, despite knowing all about Superman's secret life as a shy reporter. Factual errors are not available to explain these intuitions. And this is where the real problem with simple sentences lies.

1.2.3 Simple sentences and Naïve Millians

Simple sentences in which substitution appears to fail pose a challenge to those who oppose a Naïve Millian view of belief reporting. However, this challenge does not show that Naïve Millianism is the right theory to hold. Nor does it show, more specifically, that Salmon and Soames's Naïve Implicature view is correct.[28]

Indeed, the Naïve Implicature view also faces challenges from simple sentences. In some ways, these challenges are not as daunting, since Naïve Implicature theorists—unlike their opponents—are already in the business of explaining away anti-substitution intuitions. Nonetheless, simple sentences provide them with new anti-substitution intuitions to explain. As it stands, Naïve Implicature theory does not yet explain anti-substitution intuitions about simple sentences. The account Naïve

---

[28] As Stefano Predelli (1999) rightly notes, the idea of providing an implicature account of simple sentences intuitions is 'little more than a research program' (p. 114). Predelli wrongly takes this to be a problem for the challenge that I pose for opponents of Naïve Implicature theory. That challenge does not rely on the idea that we already have a well-worked out implicature-based account of simple sentence intuitions. It is right, however, to insist that Naïve Implicature theorists owe us an explanation of simple sentence intuitions. I explore their possibilities for doing so in Chapter 3.

Implicature theorists have offered of anti-substitution intuitions about propositional attitude reporting sentences is just that: an account of intuitions about *propositional attitude reporting* sentences. The same is true of attempts to further flesh out their sketchy explanations. An account that confines itself solely to explaining intuitions about attitude-reporting sentences cannot be said to explain intuitions about non-attitude-reporting sentences.

Naïve Implicature theorists, like the other theorists we have discussed, do have a way of explaining some anti-substitution intuitions regarding simple sentences: those of the unenlightened. For Nathan Salmon (11) and (11*) express the same proposition.

(11) Clark Kent went into the phone booth and Superman came out.
(11*) Superman went into the phone booth and Clark Kent came out.

However, these two sentences present the proposition under different guises. One who is unaware of the double life will fail to recognise that the same proposition is being presented in different ways. The difference in guises may affect her truth-conditional intuitions. Thus, she may fail to realise that the sentences cannot differ in truth value.[29] As we have seen with other accounts, though, explaining the intuitions of the unenlightened is the easy part. To properly deal with the difficulties posed by simple sentences, one must also explain the intuitions of the enlightened. Doing this would require, at the very least, some extension of implicature explanations of attitude reporting intuitions.[30] It is not immediately obvious how to do this, since any accounts of these intuitions will postulate implicatures that arise from attitude reporting sentences, and simple sentences are by definition not attitude reporting sentences.

Naïve Millians more generally—rather than just Naïve Implicature theorists—face the same sorts of problems. Although explaining away anti-substitution intuitions about simple sentences fits more naturally with their theoretical outlook than it does with the outlook of those who oppose Naïve Millianism, they must still explain them away. Simple sentences represent an extra sort of case for Naïve Millians to explain.

---

[29] The Naïve Implicature theorist, then, need not use implicatures to explain *all* anti-substitution intuitions. (For more on this move, see Braun 1998.) On the other hand, she could do so. Rather than adopting the simple explanation above, she could instead insist that even the intuitions of the unenlightened are to be explained via implicatures. Because I find this version of the view needlessly complex, I do not discuss it here.

[30] Eventually—in Chapter 3— I will argue that this cannot be done.

In short, simple sentences that appear to resist substitution of co-referential names are a problem for everyone. In the chapters that follow, I show that the problem is not one that is easily solved. After discussing many attempted solutions that fail, I argue that simple sentences indicate a need for a new approach to our truth-conditional intuitions.

2

Simple Sentences and Semantics

The last chapter introduced us to the problems that apparently substitution-resistant simple sentences pose for standard approaches to substitution puzzle cases. In particular, it showed us that it is far from obvious how traditional theories can be adapted to cover these new cases, which do not involve any of the constructions standardly blamed for substitution failure (or its appearance). This chapter explores the prospects for semantic theories that uphold our truth-conditional intuitions about simple sentences.[1] Broadly speaking, these theories come in two varieties: those that don't allow for substantial contextual variation in truth conditions and those that do. I argue that those who wish to uphold our intuitions should prefer an account allowing for contextual variation. But although such accounts have much better prospects than those without contextual variation, they also fail, for very important reasons. These reasons, the Enlightenment Problem and the Aspect Problem, are quite general difficulties raised by simple sentences, rather than simply objections to particular accounts. We will see that they arise over and over again in subsequent chapters as we explore further approaches to simple sentences. In the end, they will be an important part of the motivation for the new approach to intuitions that I suggest.

Before I begin my look at these accounts, I should say a word or two about terminology. In what follows, I frequently refer to 'anti-substitution intuitions'. As we will see, however, some accounts designed to accommodate what I have called 'anti-substitution intuitions' have the result that no substitution of co-referential names takes place in (1) and (1*).

(1) Superman leaps more tall buildings than Clark Kent does.
(1*) Superman leaps more tall buildings than Superman does.

---

[1] A reminder: I use the phrase 'truth conditions' to refer to the truth values of a sentence in a context, evaluated both at the actual world and at other possible worlds. Truth-conditional intuitions are intuitions about these truth values.

On these accounts, the terms 'Clark Kent' and 'Superman', ordinarily taken to be co-referential, are—in at least some contexts—not co-referential. Since the intuitions I am discussing are pre-theoretical, however, and since pre-theoretically we take the terms 'Superman' and 'Clark Kent' to name the same individual, I will for convenience persist in calling the intuitions 'anti-substitution intuitions'. Nothing hangs on this terminological decision.

2.1 ACCOUNTS WITHOUT CONTEXTUAL VARIATION

One simple way to block substitution in sentences like (1) and (1*) is to maintain that 'Superman' and 'Clark Kent' never refer to the same individual—we are making a mistake when we take them to do so. In fact, according to a story like this, they refer to different things. An account like this will very easily give different truth values to (1) and (1*), and it can make sense of (1)'s truth: *of course* one thing may leap more tall buildings than another thing. This account, then, honours our anti-substitution intuitions about simple sentences. However, this account also has the result that (2) must be false.

(2) Superman is Clark Kent.

But surely one of our strongest intuitions about the Superman/Clark story is that (2) is true. To insist that (2) is simply false, then, is a bad strategy for one who hopes to uphold intuitions.

A further problem comes with trying to figure out just what the different things referred to by 'Superman' and 'Clark Kent' are. One obvious candidate is temporal parts (or collections of temporal parts). Approaches like this bring with them further difficulties.

2.1.1 A simple temporal part account

One easy way to get some of the desired results is to take the names 'Superman' and 'Clark Kent' to refer to different temporal parts of the same individual. 'Superman' names the superhero bits of Superman/Clark Kent, while 'Clark' names the reporter bits. Since there is a lot of shifting back and forth between the superhero and the reporter, each name must be a name for a discontinuous collection of temporal parts. Although it might well prove difficult to cash this out in detail, let's assume that it can be made to work. 'Superman' and 'Clark Kent', then, refer to distinct collections of temporal parts. The names 'Superman' and 'Clark Kent', then, do not co-refer. (1) and (1*) may differ in truth value because different temporal parts are referred to—and different temporal parts of the same individual are not guaranteed to do the same thing. One may go into a phone booth, and another may emerge. And with different collections of temporal parts being picked out by the two names, there is nothing puzzling about the apparent truth of (1).[2]

As we already noted, an account like this will have the consequence that (2) is false. But temporal parts theorists do have ways of making such identity sentences come out true. In particular they may understand the 'is' in (2) as expressing 'is a part of the same thing as'. On this reading (2) should really be understood along the lines of (2TP)

(2TP) Superman is a part of the same thing as Clark Kent.

(2TP) is, of course, true. If (2) is to be understood as (2TP), then, temporal parts theorists can uphold the truth of (2).

But identity sentences will not be the only problematic ones. Suppose that Kevin has just learned that 'Superman' and 'Clark' name the same individual. This shocks him, and he starts working out the implications of it. Kevin utters (3).

(3) Astounding—Superman spends a lot of time acting shy and nerdy!

(3) seems true. But it cannot be, on the simple temporal part account: those time slices named by 'Superman' never act shy and nerdy.[3]

It may also be difficult to work out exactly which temporal parts are picked out by which name. Some cases will be clear enough—the hero, flying to the scene of the crime; or the reporter, quietly taking notes. But others will be less clear—is it Superman or Clark Kent taking a shower by himself?

---

[2] There is nothing puzzling, that is, assuming that we can make sense of the idea that collections of temporal parts leap buildings.

[3] Perhaps the temporal parts theorist could reconstrue (3) as something like (3TP): *Astounding—Superman is a part of a thing that spends a lot of time acting shy and nerdy!* But how would this view go? Would all claims involving double-life cases be reconstrued in such a way? If so, (1) would need to be reconstrued as something like (1TP): *Superman is a part of a thing that leaps more tall buildings than the thing of which Clark Kent is a part.* But (1TP) is false, so the revised version of the temporal parts view would fail to accord with the very intuitions that motivate the view in the first place. Perhaps a way could be found to apply this sort of reconstrual in only some cases, blocking substitution only where intuition demands. If this is done, however, the view begins to incorporate quite substantial context-dependence. Views with this sort of context-dependence will be dealt with shortly.

A further problem comes with an example first discussed by Joseph Moore (1999). Suppose, he suggests, that Clark/Superman is sitting at his desk dressed as Clark and talking on the phone to Lois as Superman. Lois looks out her window and sees Clark during the conversation. We might report this truthfully by uttering (4):

(4) While talking on the phone to Superman, Lois looked through the window at Clark Kent.

Nonetheless, an utterance of (4*) would seem false:

(4*) While talking on the phone to Superman, Lois looked through the window at Superman.

A temporal part view cannot make sense of this apparent difference—at any one time, only one temporal part will be present. She cannot be talking on the phone to one temporal part and at *the same time* looking at a different one. If (4) is true, then, (4*) must be as well. An account that simply takes 'Clark Kent' and 'Superman' to refer to different temporal parts, then, is inadequate.

2.1.2 Pitt's view: alter and primum egos

David Pitt (2001) offers an account that makes use of temporal parts, but in a more complicated way than the simple view sketched above. Pitt claims that what is at work in the problematic simple sentence cases is actually the complex phenomenon of individuals with alter egos. Alter egos, for Pitt, are collections of temporal parts of individuals. According to him, the names 'Superman' and 'Clark Kent' are not co-referential names, and neither are certain other pairs of names standardly considered co-referential, such as 'Bruce Wayne' and 'Batman'. Take 'Bruce Wayne' and 'Batman' first. Bruce Wayne should be understood as a man who decided to make himself a costume and fight crime under a new persona. He is, then, an individual with an alter ego, Batman. Since the individual Bruce Wayne has an alter ego, he can be understood as a *primum ego* (individuals without alters are not primum egos.) The primum ego is still present even when the alter ego is. According to Pitt, anything Batman does Bruce Wayne does, because he is Bruce Wayne *occupying* the Batman persona. But Batman does not do everything Bruce Wayne does, because sometimes Bruce Wayne isn't using that persona. The case of Superman is different. 'Superman' and 'Clark Kent' are names for two alter-egos that the alien Kal-El adopted on Earth.

Kal-El does everything either Superman or Clark does, and some things that neither of them do.

Such a view, like the simple temporal part view discussed above, can easily claim a difference in truth value between (1) and (1*).

(1) Superman leaps more tall buildings than Clark Kent.
(1*) Superman leaps more tall buildings than Superman.

If the names 'Superman' and 'Clark Kent' refer to different alter-egos, there is no difficulty assigning different truth values to these sentences. Unfortunately, this account also shares the key weaknesses of the simple temporal part view. First, the example from Moore, above, shows that temporal parts are not fine-grained enough to capture all of our intuitions. Pitt needs to be able to answer the question of which persona Kal-El is occupying when he is making eye contact with Lois as Clark while speaking to her on the phone as Superman; and he needs his answer to provide intuitively correct truth conditions for (4) and (4*).

(4) While talking on the phone to Superman, Lois looked through the window at Clark Kent.
(4*) While talking on the phone to Superman, Lois looked through the window at Superman.

Pitt cannot provide such intuitively correct truth conditions, since it is the same temporal part that is talking to Lois and being looked at by her.

Next, Pitt's account gives the very counter-intuitive result that (2) and (3) below are false.

(2) Superman is Clark Kent.
(3) Astounding—Superman spends a lot of time acting shy and nerdy!

Similarly for sentence (5), as alter-egos are not the same as the individuals (primum egos) who have alter egos.

(5) Superman is Kal-El.

Pitt realises that some will find it counterintuitive to claim that identity sentences like (2) and (5) are false. But he urges that the reason many people wrongly (according to him) take a claim like (2) to be true is that they understand it as 'meaning the same as' (2P) below (Pitt 2001: 544).

(2) Superman is Clark Kent.
(2P) The person whose alter ego is Superman is the person whose alter ego is Clark Kent.

Pitt's explanation seems to me unlikely. One clear reason to worry about it is the fact that most of us—myself included, until I read Pitt's paper—have forgotten (if we ever knew) that there is a third name involved with Superman/Clark Kent's double life—'Kal-El'. We have forgotten, that is, that there is some individual who (in Pitt's terminology) adopted two alter egos, those of Superman and Clark Kent. We will not, then, think that there is some individual who has both of these alter egos. (It is more likely, though still not uncontentious, that we would take Clark Kent to have the alter ego Superman.) So it just doesn't make sense to suppose that we understand (2) as meaning what (2P) does: most of us just aren't in a position to do this. Pitt's explanation seems even more problematic when we consider that he is committed to different sorts of explanations for the intuitive truth of different identity sentences. Take, for example, (6).

(6) Bruce Wayne is Batman.

Because Bruce Wayne is not an alter ego, but an individual who *adopted* an alter ego, when we falsely take (6) to be true it is because we understand it as meaning the same as (6P) below.

(6P) Bruce Wayne is the person whose alter ego is Batman.

If this is right, then we understand (2) and (6) in such a way as to attribute very different structures to them. (2) and (6) appear superficially to have the same simple structure—that of identity sentences. But, according to Pitt, we tend to understand (2) as making reference to three entities—two alter egos and a person. And we tend to understand (6) as making reference only to one person and his alter ego. But it really doesn't seem like we do this—the sentences seem to us to have the same structure. Pitt's explanation cannot succeed unless he can plausibly maintain that we understand (2) as (2P) and (6) as (6P). But this seems counterintuitive.

The differences in Pitt's treatments of the Bruce Wayne/Batman and Superman/Clark Kent stories lead to another problem as well. Suppose that, in Clark Kent-mode, Kal-El got in one fight, and that he has been in many fights in Superman-mode. (7) would then be false.

(7) Clark Kent has been in more fights than Superman.

And this result seems right—it certainly seems that Superman is more of a fighter than Clark. Suppose that, while not in Bat-mode, Bruce

Wayne got in one fight, and that he has been in many fights in Bat-mode. For Pitt, this must be treated very differently, because 'Bruce Wayne'—unlike 'Clark Kent'—is the name of a primum ego. As a result, everything Batman does is something that Bruce Wayne does (but not vice versa). (8), then, is true.

(8) Bruce Wayne has been in more fights than Batman.

It seems to me counterintuitive to claim that (8) is true. But, perhaps more importantly, it seems counterintuitive to treat (7) and (8) so differently from one another. Intuitively, the cases are alike. But the machinery of primum and alter egos requires that they be treated differently.

Finally, Pitt's account relies entirely on the notion of individuals inhabiting personae—something like roles—that they have created. An account like this is ill-equipped to deal with substitution failures involving names that are clearly not names for agents or their alter egos. St Petersburg has not created an alter ego, Leningrad; nor has Leningrad created St Petersburg as alter ego. For Pitt, then, (9) and (9*) must take the same truth value.

(9) I visited St Petersburg once, but I never made it to Leningrad.
(9*) I visited St Petersburg once, but I never made it to St Petersburg.

But it is very difficult to see, intuitively, why (9) and (9*) must both be false, while (10) may be true—as it may be, for Pitt.

(10) He hit Clark Kent once, but he never hit Superman.

Pitt's account, then, violates quite a lot of our intuitions about simple sentences. Since it is motivated by a desire to uphold our intuitions, this is very problematic.[4]

2.2 ACCOUNTS WITH CONTEXTUAL VARIATION

It is possible to avoid some of the counterintuitive results noted above by offering an account of simple sentences on which their truth conditions may vary with context (beyond the usual variation in reference of indexicals and so on). Such contextual variation makes room for the

---

[4] I raised these objections in Saul (2001) reply to Pitt at the Pacific Division APA. Stefano Predelli (2004) raises some other excellent objections, as well as some of the same ones that I raise here.

idea that in one context, 'Superman sometimes acts shy and nerdy' may be true while in another context it may be false—without any difference in the facts about Superman's behaviour. Contextual variation also makes room for the possibility that the identity sentence 'Superman is Clark Kent' might be true even though substitution of the names 'Superman' and 'Clark' can fail. If the goal is that of finding an account that vindicates all of our intuitions about simple sentences, a context-dependent account looks like the best hope. (The accounts discussed below happen not to make use of temporal parts. There is no reason that there couldn't be a context-dependent temporal part view, but there also seems no reason to suppose that it would escape the problems outlined below.)

The views I discuss below—from Joseph Moore, Graeme Forbes, and Stefano Predelli—all have the result that in some contexts substitution will succeed in simple sentences while in other contexts it will not. Moore's and Forbes's views are importantly similar, while Predelli's is quite different, so I will save it for last.

As we have seen, names like 'Superman' and 'Clark Kent' *do* sometimes seem to do just what they've always been taken to do in simple sentences—they do sometimes seem to simply pick out individuals, as in a typical utterance of (3):

(3) Astounding—Superman spends a lot of time acting shy and nerdy!

On the other hand, simple sentences in which substitution seems to fail to motivate the thought that something else is going on semantically in other cases.[5] What makes the difference? We will discuss this in far more detail later, and it will in fact prove to be very problematic. But it is worth having in mind a broad outline of the answer that Moore and Forbes will give. According to them, what makes the difference is the conversational participants. Conversational participants who know that 'Superman' and 'Clark Kent' co-refer will sometimes want to say something that isn't just about the individuals—as when such a person utters (1).

(1) Superman leaps more tall buildings than Clark Kent.

When people like this utter (1), substitution may fail. But, according to both Forbes and Moore, this will never happen if conversational

---

[5] As we will see, Predelli insists that names never do anything but pick out their referents—yet nonetheless his account assigns contextually varying truth conditions to simple sentences in such a way as to allow substitution to be blocked in many cases.

participants are not aware of the double life—it simply wouldn't occur to them to talk about anything other than individuals. In such cases, the names never do anything but refer to individuals (in simple sentences). Substitution, then, must succeed. Moore and Forbes call those who know about the double life 'the enlightened' and those who don't 'the unenlightened'. Substitution, for them, may only fail when enlightened conversational participants are deliberately discussing something other than just individuals. The rest of the time, substitution must succeed.

2.2.1 Forbes's and Moore's views

Graeme Forbes's (1997, 1999) and Joseph Moore's (1999) are similar, we've seen, in allowing for contextual variation regarding what proposition is expressed by an utterance of a simple sentence. They are also similar in taking this variation to depend on what the conversational participants are trying to talk about—individuals or *something else*. But their views differ when it comes to just what this something else is (as well as in many smaller ways).

For Moore, the key to getting the truth conditions right for simple sentences is that names sometimes refer to individuals and sometimes to what he calls 'aspects' of those individuals. Utterances of sentences (11) and (11*) may differ in truth value, because, in typical utterances, the names 'Superman' and 'Clark' will refer not to the single individual Superman/Clark but rather to the different aspects named by 'Superman' and 'Clark'.

(11) Clark Kent went into the phone booth, and Superman came out.
(11*) Superman went into the phone booth, and Clark Kent came out.

That is, (11) and (11*) will most likely express propositions that can be roughly captured by (11M) and (11*M):

(11M) Superman/Clark's Clark Kent-aspect went into the phone booth, and Superman/Clark's Superman-aspect came out.
(11*M) Superman/Clark's Superman-aspect went into the phone booth, and Superman/Clark's Clark Kent-aspect came out.[6]

---

[6] Although the formulations in (11M) and (11*M)—*Superman/Clark's Superman-aspect, Superman/Clark's Clark-aspect*—are the ones that Moore uses, they may be slightly misleading. They seem to suggest that Superman/Clark, the individual, plays a role in the propositions Moore takes (11) and (11*) to express when the express aspect-sensitive propositions. This is wrong—for Moore, it is only the aspect, not the individual, that makes it into such propositions.

Utterances of the identity sentence (2), on the other hand, will typically be true:

(2) Superman is Clark Kent.

In utterances of (2), the names 'Superman' and 'Clark' will generally refer to the individual and not to aspects of him. For Moore, then, one key move consists in the fact that the names 'Superman' and 'Clark' are only *sometimes* co-referential.

Graeme Forbes achieves similar results via a somewhat different mechanism.[7] For him, propositions expressed by simple sentences always include reference to individuals, and the names 'Superman' and 'Clark' co-refer. Yet Forbes manages to block substitution in some utterances of simple sentences by claiming that sometimes the sentences will express propositions that are partly about what he calls 'modes of personification'.[8] Utterances of (11) and (11*), for example, will typically express propositions roughly captured by (11F) and (11*F) below.

(11F) Clark Kent, so-personified, went into the phone booth, and Superman, so-personified, came out.
(11*F) Superman, so-personified, went into the phone booth, and Clark Kent, so-personified, came out.

The 'so' in 'so-personified' is an indexical that refers to the name preceding it. Thus 'Clark Kent, so-personified' can be understood as, roughly, *Clark Kent/Superman, under his 'Clark Kent'-labelled mode of personification*. The labels 'Clark Kent' and 'Superman' attach to different modes of personification. Importantly, modes of personification are not individuated temporally—Superman may be personified in more than one way at the same time. To get this result, Forbes employs a semantics of adverbial modification: 'If Clark was personified in two ways at *t*, then there were two events *e1* and *e2* such that in *e1*, Clark was personified in one of the ways while perhaps satisfying a condition *C*, and in *e2* Clark was personified in a different way while perhaps satisfying the

---

[7] Forbes's account of simple sentences is an accompaniment to his account of propositional attitude reporting (Forbes 1990, 1993) and his account of intensional transitives (2002). The accounts of attitude reporting and intensional transitives use the more familiar modes of presentation, rather than modes of personification.

[8] It may be worth noting that some modes of personification do not concern persons. Forbes is clear that he takes non-persons like Leningrad/St Petersburg to have modes of personification.

contradictory condition not-C' (Forbes 1999: 90). Forbes, then, avoids the problems that come with temporal parts.[9]

Because of the different modes of personification involved, (11F) and (11*F) may easily differ in truth value. Sometimes, however, the propositions expressed by simple sentences do not include modes of personification. This is what allows Forbes to accommodate the truth of some utterances of (3), and of the identity sentence (2).

(2) Superman is Clark Kent.
(3) Astounding—Superman spends a lot of time acting shy and nerdy!

2.2.2 Aspects and modes of personification (the Aspect Problem)

2.2.2.1 *What are they?*

Moore's and Forbes's accounts depend on the viability of the entities—aspects and modes of personification—to which they commit themselves. At first, Forbes attempted to explain modes of personification in terms of more familiar notions, like ways of dressing (Forbes 1997; Saul 1997*b*). But now he simply insists that the notion of modes of personification is quite a commonsense one that needs very little explanation. Forbes means to show that we already understand and are committed to modes of personification, even if we do not have a workable detailed analysis of them:

A certain extraterrestrial leads a double life. In one life, he must conceal the fact that he comes from another planet, that he has extraordinary powers, and so on. In the other life, he must at least conceal the existence of his first life. And at the *changeover* points, he must be careful not to be observed. This much is obvious, and shows that we have the conception of a single individual who puts on one performance for some stretches of his life and a different performance for others. (Forbes 1999: 89)

This, according to Forbes, is all that we need to be committed to in order to be committed to modes of personification. But I am not sure that it suffices. First, a quibble: not all double life cases involve *concealment*. Sam Clemens did nothing to *conceal* his life as Mark Twain. This is, however, inessential to Forbes's description. What seems far more central is his notion of *performance*. And this proves very problematic

---

[9] Thomas Ede Zimmerman (2005: 67–8), however, has raised some interesting problems for Forbes's use of events.

for some simple sentence cases: Forbes needs the names 'Leningrad' and 'St Petersburg' to serve as labels for modes of personification, and performances by the city don't seem to play any role in the difference between these purported modes of personification.

Moore's aspects are somewhat different. Where Forbes's modes of personification are ways that individuals may be presented, Moore's aspects are actually entities that can walk, talk, and leap tall buildings. But Moore also insists that aspects are commonsensical, in the sense that he takes our pre-theoretical ontology to be committed to them. He writes:

Aspects are, I think, primitive, irreducible, and, as I shall suggest shortly, somewhat indeterminate[10] entities. Our pre-reflective conceptual scheme demands them, but the scheme alone doesn't decisively answer certain philosophical questions about them. We can usefully model an aspect as a collection of properties of a certain type (or, alternatively, as a complex property that conjoins these properties) . . . the aspect associated with a name in a context instantiates the properties associated with the name by the conversation's participants. (Moore 1999: 103)

Once more, I am not so sure about the commonsensicality of aspects. One way to see this is to consider the way that Moore describes them in the passage above, in combination with the work Moore needs them to do. Moore needs aspects to be the sorts of things that can walk into phone booths, hit people, leap tall buildings, and so on. But, as he himself notes (1999: 103n), collections of properties can't do these things. His response to this is to emphasise his claim that we only *model* aspects as collections of properties—obviously, he notes, they've got to be something else. But what? If the best model we can come up with for aspects is one that clearly fails to capture key features of them, it is natural to wonder if something is amiss. Those who find aspects completely commonsensical will perhaps not be worried by this. But for those with doubts, it is a troubling feature. And surely doubt is reasonable: it is by no means clear that our commonsense ontology is committed to *aspects*. Perhaps we are committed to *something* that can do the sort of job that Moore's aspects or Forbes's modes of personification can do (though I

[10] Moore invokes indeterminacy to deal with cases in which the truth conditions for simple sentences are, intuitively, indeterminate. His example is one in which Clark enters a 'phone booth dressed as Clark and emerges in purple swimming trunks' (Moore 1999: 104). As Moore notes, we will intuitively assign an indeterminate truth value to (11) in this situation—unless we have a view about which aspect wears purple swimming trunks.

am doubtful even about this idea). But why insist that it is *aspects* that we are committed to? It seems very hard for Moore to maintain that it is—especially since the best model of them he can offer is one at odds with what he takes them to be. Neither Moore nor Forbes, then, has offered us a fully satisfying story about the theoretical entities that are so important to their accounts.[11]

2.2.2.2 *How are they picked out?*

Even if we did feel that aspects or modes of personification were commonsense entities, there would be further questions to answer about them. In particular, we need to know which ones make it into which propositions. Even if we knew what aspects were, we would still need to know what the Superman-aspect is. Even if we knew what modes of personification were, we would need to know what the 'Clark Kent' mode of personification is. We need to know these things in order to know whether Moore's and Forbes's accounts really do succeed in accommodating our truth-conditional intuitions about simple sentences. It turns out, as we will see in this section, that these questions are far more difficult to answer than one might have thought. Without satisfying answers, however, Forbes and Moore cannot claim to have offered accounts that capture our intuitions.

2.2.2.2.1 Moore

Moore writes of 'Superman-aspects' and 'Clark-aspects'. These are, for him, the aspects associated with the names 'Superman' and 'Clark' respectively. Moore clarifies further: 'the aspect associated with the name in a context instantiates the properties associated with the name by the conversation's participants' (Moore 1999: 103). This characterisation, it seems to me, yields very problematic results. To see why, we need to consider some examples.

---

[11] One might object that I am holding aspects/modes of personification to an unfairly high standard. We don't worry about our ability to refer to, for example, Tony Blair just because we lack a satisfying theory of what individuals are. So, the objection goes, we should not question our ability to refer to a Superman-aspect just because we lack a satisfying theory of what an aspect is. But the situations are not at all parallel. With the exception of a few philosophers, we are all very strongly committed, pretheoretically, to the existence of things like Tony Blair, and we would all freely admit as much. This is not at all the case when it comes to such things as Superman-aspects, recently proposed theoretical entities that most people have never explicitly considered, and which require quite a bit of explanation.

Imagine that Alfred and Betty, both fully aware of Clark's double life, are discussing his antics. Alfred utters (1).

(1) Superman leaps more tall buildings than Clark Kent.

Alfred means to be discussing aspects, and Betty knows this. Alfred, then, has said something like (1M).

(1M) The Superman-aspect leaps more tall buildings than the Clark Kent-aspect.

But which aspect is the Superman-aspect? It will be the one that instantiates the properties Alfred and Betty associate with 'Superman'. Now, however, imagine that whenever Betty has seen Superman, he has worn his traditional cape. Alfred, however, has only seen Superman wearing his post-1997 cape-free ensemble,[12] and he has been struck by the fact that the Man of Steel does not bother with the by-now-cliched superhero cape. Betty will associate with 'Superman' the property *wears a cape* and Alfred will associate with 'Superman' the property *doesn't wear a cape*. (Neither of them has any reason to think there have been costume changes, so they don't include reference to time in the costume-related properties they associate with 'Superman'.) These properties are incompatible, so no aspect whatsoever is picked out. The result of this, it would seem, is that Alfred—attempting but failing to express an aspect-sensitive proposition—has made an utterance with no truth value. Intuitively, however, Alfred and Betty's slight disagreement should make no difference to truth value. Those who think Alfred's utterance is true will not be inclined to change their minds on learning that Betty has failed to keep up with Superman's changing fashion statements.

One way to deal with such disagreements is to allow for the possibility that Alfred and Betty may pick out different aspects by their utterances of 'Superman'. Alfred picks out an aspect that doesn't wear a cape, while Betty picks out an aspect that does. It is easy to see how both sorts of aspects could exist if aspects were collections of time-slices—Alfred and Betty would simply pick out different, non-overlapping temporal parts. Moore does not take aspects to be collections of temporal parts, however; and, as I have noted, it is somewhat unclear just what he takes them to be. Nonetheless, it does not seem impossible for him to claim

---

[12] For more on the big costume change, see Moos (1997).

that both of these aspects exist, and that Alfred picks out one and Betty the other.

This solution, however, brings with it its own problems. First, it has the result that Alfred and Betty express different propositions when they utter (1), even though they are both focusing on aspects. Whenever they converse about Superman in hero-mode, moreover, they will talk past each other—Alfred will speak of one aspect, and Betty will understand him as referring to a different one. This problem becomes especially acute when we consider what happens if Betty reports what Alfred said when he uttered (1). Suppose that Betty utters (1R):

(1R) Alfred said that Superman leaps more tall buildings than Clark Kent.

Betty's report seems to us a perfectly accurate one. But for Moore, Betty's utterance (1R) must be false. When Alfred uttered (1), 'Superman' picked out a different aspect from the one that it picks out in Betty's utterance. Alfred did not express anything about the aspect that *Betty* associates with 'Superman', so her report (1R) cannot be true. This seems very counterintuitive.

Another response one could try would be to simply accept an indeterminacy in what aspect is picked out by 'Superman'. There are various ways that one might deal with such an indeterminacy. One would be to accept an indeterminacy in truth value as well. But this seems unlikely to be acceptable: Alfred's utterance of (1) just seems true. However, one could also maintain that (1) is true despite the indeterminacy—because *either* of the aspects in question leap more tall buildings than the one picked out by 'Clark Kent'.

But while this second version of the indeterminacy response is fine as far as the truth value of (1) goes, it is not so acceptable when it comes to indirect speech reports. Imagine that Alfred, once again, utters (1) to Betty.

(1) Superman leaps more tall buildings than Clark Kent.

Because Alfred and Betty have different aspects in mind, it is indeterminate what 'Superman' refers to, and so indeterminate what proposition is expressed by (1). Now Betty reports Alfred's utterance with (1R), in a conversation with Caleb.

(1R) Alfred said that Superman leaps more tall buildings than Clark Kent.

But Caleb, like Betty (and unlike Alfred) associates the property *wears a cape* with 'Superman'. There is no disagreement whatsoever between

Betty and Caleb over what properties to associate with 'Superman'. In Betty and Caleb's conversation, then, 'Superman' determinately picks out an aspect that wears a cape. In other words, it makes a very different contribution to the proposition expressed by Betty's utterance of (1R) than it did to the proposition expressed by Alfred's utterance of (1). Betty's utterance of (1R) can only be true if Alfred expressed a determinate proposition which included the cape-wearing aspect of Superman. But he did no such thing. So, on this view, her utterance of (1R) must be false. But this seems wrong: Betty's utterance was clearly true, and a disagreement over cape-wearing should not undermine this.

A further problem comes in if we imagine that, by some fluke, Superman only happened to leap tall buildings when he was wearing a cape. If this is the case, then the indeterminacy becomes even more problematic: one choice of Superman-aspect does indeed leap more tall buildings than the 'Clark' aspect—but the other does not. We cannot, then, insist that the utterance is true whichever aspect is the relevant one: (1) must lack a truth value. But this result just seems wrong—a disagreement over exact costume surely should not affect truth value in this way.

2.2.2.2.2 Forbes

Forbes tells a slightly different story. For Forbes, the 'Clark'-labelled mode of personification will be the one that 'others' associate with 'Clark': Forbes writes that 'attired in the "Clark Kent" way' refers to 'the style Clark is affecting in situations where others apply "Clark" to him' (Forbes 1997: 111). Moore took the 'Clark'-labelled aspect to be the one with the *properties* conversational participants associate with 'Clark'. Forbes's view is simpler—the only relevant property for him will be that of being labeled 'Clark', by 'others'.

It is not entirely clear whom it is that Forbes takes the relevant 'others' to be—unlike Moore, he does not say that they must be the conversational participants. First, suppose that Forbes is requiring that *all* others associate this mode of personification with 'Clark'. Clearly, this is too strong: some people are unenlightened and do not associate any modes of personification with 'Clark'. (Such people think that Clark is simply an individual like any other, and that there's no need to ever consider modes of personification.) This would presumably have the result that no mode of personification is associated with 'Clark'—there would be no mode of personification that meets the condition of being associated with 'Clark' by everyone. The result of this on Forbes's semantics would be a little unclear: one option is to say that 'Clark' only ever picks out an individual—try as they might, people only ever express propositions about individuals when they use the name 'Clark'. (The same will of course be true of 'Superman'.) On this option, (1) must be false, clearly an undesirable result for Forbes.

(1) Superman leaps more tall buildings than Clark Kent.

The other option would be to maintain that when we try to express mode-of-presentation-containing propositions by using the name 'Clark', we simply express propositions with gaps in them where modes of personification should be. This would presumably mean that (1) has no truth value, still not a good result for Forbes.

Forbes is more likely to mean that the 'Clark'-labelled mode of personification will be the one that all *enlightened* people associate with 'Clark'. This is, however, still too strong. To see this, consider an utterance of (1) in a new conversation, between Candy and Desmond.

(1) Superman leaps more tall buildings than Clark Kent.

Candy and Desmond are both enlightened, and they associate all the same properties with 'Superman' and 'Clark'. But recall that Alfred and Betty (participants in a completely separate conversation) are also among the enlightened. Yet Betty thinks that Superman wore a cape for his heroic exploits while Alfred thinks that he didn't. In order to avoid the problem that Moore faced, Forbes needs to claim that, somehow, both of them associate the same mode of personification with 'Superman'—otherwise there won't be just one mode of presentation that the enlightened associate with 'Superman'. But it's just not clear how he can maintain this: after all, Alfred thinks that Superman defied super-peer-pressure by refusing to wear a cape. If presented with a photo of Superman in a cape, Alfred would say 'No, that's not Superman—he'd never wear that'. The most natural description of the situation is that Betty associates 'Superman' with a mode of personification that includes wearing a cape, while Alfred associates 'Superman' with a mode of personification that does not include this. This would mean that no single mode of personification is picked out by 'Superman'. The result of this for Forbes's account, following the reasoning in the previous paragraph, is that utterances of (1) are either false or lacking in truth value—even though Alfred and Betty are no part of the conversation. And, as we have seen, this is not a desirable result. Any difference of opinion among the enlightened regarding what counts as a 'Superman' mode of personification would lead to this outcome. Among *all* the people aware of a particular double life there are likely to be at least some disagreements of the relevant sort. So the problem Forbes faces on this understanding of his account would be both serious and widespread.

Taking the relevant 'others' to be just the conversational participants reduces but does not eliminate the problem. The problem is reduced, because now Alfred and Betty's disagreement does not affect what is said in conversations of which they are not a part. But it is not eliminated, because the problem of their own conversation remains. If Alfred and Betty associate different modes of personification with 'Superman', then Forbes needs to explain what propositions their utterances of (1) express in conversation with one another. One possible consequence of this is that their utterances must be either false or lacking in truth value, but we have seen that Forbes should want to avoid this. Another option, also previously explored (in our discussion of Moore) is to maintain that Alfred and Betty express different propositions in their utterances of (1)—the proposition expressed by Alfred's utterance is about one mode of personification and the proposition expressed by Betty's utterance is about another. But this seems unintuitive—it means that Alfred and Betty will fail to grasp the propositions expressed by each others' utterances, and that when Betty tries to report on what Alfred has said in his utterance of (1), she will be doomed to failure.

Forbes could, however, attempt to describe the situation differently: he might maintain that although Alfred and Betty associate different properties with 'Superman', and would make different judgments about when Superman is personified in the 'Superman' way, they in fact associate the name 'Superman' with just a single mode of personification. As a result, they express the same proposition in their utterances of (12), and they understand each other's utterances perfectly. This line could perhaps be motivated by an analogy with names—although two speakers may associate different properties with, for example, the name 'Aristotle', most theorists today have managed to offer views on which these speakers' utterances of 'Aristotle' refer to the same individual. Forbes could suggest that reference to modes of personification works much like reference to individuals, like Aristotle. But this suggestion alone is not enough. Forbes would need to offer us a theory of how reference to modes of personification works. And here is where the analogy breaks down: current theories of how 'Aristotle' refers (including Forbes's own) tend to invoke—in one way or another—causal theories of reference. The guiding idea behind this approach is that (however the details are filled in) there are causal chains connecting current utterances of 'Aristotle' to previous utterances, and eventually to Aristotle himself. Although lots of wrinkles need to be ironed out, this basic approach seems a promising one.

Causal theories do not seem so promising when it comes to modes of personification. In part, this is because individuals are common-sense entities, and common-sense is clearly committed to the idea that we causally interact with these entities. Not so for modes of personification. But if we did want to try such a causal theory, it would presumably go something like this: in, for example, Ezra's utterance of (1), 'Superman' contributes not simply Superman himself to the proposition, but Superman personified in the 'Superman' way.

(1) Superman leaps more tall buildings than Clark Kent.

The way referred to will be the one that the person who taught Ezra about the 'Superman' mode referred to when she said 'Superman'. And this will, in turn, be the mode that the person who taught *her* referred to. To make this sort of account work, we need (among other things) a single mode of personification at the start of this chain, that can be referred to again and again by people. These people will need to be referring to this same mode of personification (whatever that is), despite thinking of Superman in very different ways: perhaps one member of the chain has never seen a picture of Superman, or heard his costume described, while another doesn't know his name but has seen him flying through the sky. Moreover, the Superman mode of presentation will only *sometimes* be a part of the proposition expressed when a sentence containing 'Superman' is uttered. *Maybe* some story can be told, but it is not at all obvious how it would go. To convince us of it, Forbes would need to say much more about what modes of personification are (as well as fleshing out the details of the causal chains involved). There is no good reason for us to suppose at this point that such a causal theory would be possible. At least as things now stand, then, it cannot save Forbes from the worries raised in this section.

The problems discussed in this section concern the nature of the theoretical entities that are so crucial to Forbes's and Moore's accounts—modes of personification and aspects. These worries concern, broadly speaking, what these entities are, how we manage to talk and think about them, and how they help us to accommodate truth-conditional intuitions. I will call this collection of worries, broadly put, 'the Aspect Problem'.

2.2.3 Determinants of contextual variation and the Enlightenment Problem

The problems outlined above are serious ones. But suppose, for the moment, that we could resolve them. We also need to know what determines whether an aspect/mode of personification will be involved at all in the proposition expressed by some utterance. Forbes and Moore insist that whether or not an aspect/mode of presentation is present depends on the states of mind of the conversational participants. There are two features of the conversational participants' minds that matter: whether or not they are enlightened, and whether or not they are thinking about aspects/modes of personification. But it is less clear which conversational participants matter, and in what way. We will consider various options, and see that all suffer from serious difficulties. In the end, this will lead us to a very difficult and recurring problem for accounts of simple sentences: the Enlightenment Problem.

A terminological note: the differences between aspects and modes of personification is no longer relevant to the discussion in this chapter. It is quite cumbersome to write 'proposition involving aspects/modes of personification'. In what follows, then, I will sometimes use the term 'aspect-sensitive proposition' as a general term for propositions involving aspects *or* modes of personification. In addition, I will from now on speak of 'aspects' as a stand-in for 'aspects or modes of personification'. However, when I am specifically discussing Forbes's writing I will use 'modes of personification', as this will allow me to quote directly from him. Nothing more than terminological convenience hangs upon these choices.

2.2.3.1 Speaker intentions

A first thought is that it is the speaker who determines whether or not an aspect-sensitive proposition is expressed. In order to express an aspect-sensitive proposition, this line of thought goes, a speaker needs to be intending to talk about aspects, and she cannot do this unless she is enlightened.

This solution seems at first to provide the needed contextual variation. A speaker who has just learned of Superman/Clark's double life and utters (3) will not intend a proposition involving aspects.

(3) Astounding—Superman spends a lot of time acting shy and nerdy!

Since no aspects would be involved in this utterance of (3), the speaker would say something true. Another speaker—also aware of Superman/Clark's double life—using (11) to describe what she witnessed on a Metropolis street.

(11) Clark Kent went into the phone booth and Superman came out.

This speaker might well intend a proposition involving aspects. If she does, then the truth of (11) will not guarantee the truth of an aspect-sensitive utterance of (11*).

(11*) Superman went into the phone booth and Clark Kent came out.

(If this speaker did *not* intend aspects to be involved in what she was saying, they would not be. The truth of an utterance of (11) would then entail the truth of an utterance of (11*).) So far, then, the account looks successful.

But it faces serious problems. In particular, we don't really think speakers have this much control over what they say. There are problems even with taking speaker intentions to be the sole determinant of demonstrative reference (see, for example, Wettstein 1984; Reimer 1991), but these problems become far more severe if we take them to have this sort of control with simple sentences. To see this, recall Forbes's discussion of the commonsensicality of modes of personification:

A certain extraterrestrial leads a double life. In one life, he must conceal the fact that he comes from another planet, that he has extraordinary powers, and so on. In the other life, he must at least conceal the existence of his first life. And at the *changeover* points, he must be careful not to be observed. This much is obvious, and shows that we have the conception of a single individual who puts on one performance for some stretches of his life and a different performance for others. (Forbes 1999: 89)

If this is all that is required for someone to count as having two modes of personification, then this may happen far more frequently than one might have thought.[13] Consider the following description of a possible double-life, based upon the Lewinsky scandal during the Clinton years.

A certain White House intern leads a double life. In one life, she must conceal the fact that she visits the President in his private office at night, that she has 'improper' relations with him, and so on. In the other, she must at least conceal

---

[13] The following example is taken from Saul (1999).

the existence of her first life. And at the *changeover* points (say, entering the Oval Office on a weekend) she must be careful not to be observed.

If we can make sense of Superman's two modes of personification, surely we can make sense of Monica Lewinsky's: garden variety intern, carrying out standard tasks, and her more secret mode of personification, engaging in some non-standard ones. Clinton might even have used different names for her, depending on which role she was playing at a given time: 'Miss Lewinsky' for the garden variety intern, and 'Monica' for the woman with whom he was on more intimate terms. A story like that we've been considering would allow Clinton to exploit this fact in order to dodge allegations of lying. Consider Clinton's January 1998 press conference utterance:

(12) I did not have sexual relations with that woman, Miss Lewinsky.

It later emerged that Clinton and Lewinsky did have an improper relationship. Assume for the sake of this argument that the relationship was such as to constitute sexual relations both by commonly accepted definitions of 'sexual relations' and as Clinton understood the term.[14] Suppose also, however, that Clinton now claims that he intended to express something about the 'Miss Lewinsky' mode of personification, rather than simply the individual. If this claim is true, then, according to Forbes, Clinton's utterance is true even if he and the individual Monica Lewinsky had a sexual relationship. So, even under these circumstances, he did not lie (although he deliberately misled). But this seems wrongheaded. Clinton's intentions do not have the power to shape the actual content of his utterance in this way. This way of avoiding the charge of lying is simply not available. An account that says it is must be wrong.

It could be argued that, in the above case, Clinton simply could not form the relevant intention. Speaker intentions, one might hold, are constrained by expectations about how the audience will interpret the utterance. A speaker cannot express the proposition that p if they don't expect that the audience will take them to be expressing the proposition that p. A closely related view holds that a speaker cannot intend to express the proposition that p if they couldn't reasonably expect the audience to take them to be expressing the proposition that p. On either view, Clinton cannot intend to say something about the 'Miss

---

[14] I am not making any claims whatsoever regarding the actual nature of their relationship.

Lewinsky' mode of personification, because he knows that the audience will not take him in this way.

The problem with this response is that it still leaves the speaker far too much flexibility. To see this, modify the case a little. Imagine now that Clinton is too preoccupied with the serious business of running the country to spare much time for keeping up with public opinion about himself. Rather than reading newspapers or watching news reports, he has his advisors fill him in on what he needs to know. These advisors do not want Clinton to be upset, because they don't want him distracted from his presidential duties. So they tell him that the public really only cares about whether Clinton and Lewinsky engaged in sex acts at those times when she was playing the role of ordinary intern. (The public, they claim, think it's vital for interns to be able to remain focused on their duties and they want to know whether he distracted her while she was trying to do the filing.) Moreover, the handlers tell him, Lewinsky's two personae are widely known and much discussed. They show him fabricated news reports on her Jekyll and Hyde lifestyle. So, they tell him, all the public wants to know is whether he had sexual relations with Lewinsky while she was in the 'Miss Lewinsky' mode of personification. To us, all this seems ludicrous. But the sheltered Clinton would believe this story, and reasonably so. On either of the views discussed in the previous paragraph, then, he could form the intention to say something about a mode of personification. Nonetheless, our intuitions about the example are unaltered: we would still think that Clinton's utterance was false. This is because speaker expectations about audiences (even if we limit them to reasonable speaker expectations) are affected by speakers' beliefs and idiosyncrasies in ways that prevent them from blocking problematic cases like this one. Speakers still have too much control, if they alone are determining whether the proposition expressed by an utterance is aspect-sensitive.

2.2.3.2 *Speaker and audience*

Joseph Moore has made it clear that he would not endorse an account on which speaker intentions were the sole determinant of whether an aspect-sensitive proposition is expressed by a particular utterance. Instead, Moore suggests that this is determined by both speaker and audience:

A simple sentence can be used to assert an aspect-sensitive proposition only in what I called an 'enlightened context'—that is, a conversational scenario in which all the participants know that the sensitive names are, in standard contexts, co-referential. (Moore 2000: 251)

According to him, aspect-sensitive propositions can only be expressed if both the speaker and the audience are focusing on the relevant aspects.[15] One cannot focus on aspects, however, unless one is enlightened. The unenlightened, taking there to be two individuals named 'Superman' and 'Clark Kent' will not take aspects of individuals to be involved in the propositions expressed by sentences containing these names.

This move rules out the Clinton example. The reason for this is that, in the example as I've set it up, only Clinton (and possibly his minders) are thinking of aspects. Most of the audience for Clinton's utterance—reporters, and readers, listeners, or viewers—have no thoughts of aspects of Monica/Miss Lewinsky. In this case, the reason is not that they are unenlightened—they are well aware that one individual is named by the two names—but rather that they do not know that these names are ever used as names for distinct aspects of the one individual. In other cases, speakers may fail to express aspect-sensitive propositions because they are speaking to an unenlightened audience.

Nonetheless, requiring both audience and speaker to be focusing on aspects (and therefore to be enlightened) seems to me to bring with it unintuitive consequences. One sort of unintuitive consequence can be seen from considering speakers who unwittingly address unenlightened audiences. Consider an enlightened speaker, Edna, striving to be truthful. She utters (13):

(13) Clark Kent went into the phone booth, and he never came out—Superman came out instead.

She fails to realise that the person she is addressing, Frieda, is unenlightened. Because her audience doesn't know about Superman's double life, Edna's utterance is not true. But this just seems wrong. The truth of Edna's utterance should not depend in this way upon her audience's state of mind. It would seem utterly misguided to tell Edna that what she said wasn't true, but that she might be able to make the same utterance truthfully if she first told Frieda about Superman's double life.

Things seem even more problematic if we consider large and non-uniform audiences. Suppose Edna is addressing an auditorium

---

[15] It is not clear to me whether Forbes would endorse this requirement. He certainly does require the speaker to be enlightened, but it is less clear that he requires the audience to be enlightened. See Forbes (1999: 88).

containing 5000 people that she takes to be enlightened, and she again utters (13). Suppose, moreover, that she is mostly right: 4999 of the people in the room are enlightened and 1 is unenlightened. The 4999 enlightened people are focusing on aspects. Nonetheless, Edna's utterance cannot be true—Moore requires that *all* the conversational participants be enlightened. Edna's utterance would, however, have been true if that 1 unenlightened person had left the room briefly, perhaps to make a phone call, just as Edna uttered (13). This just seems bizarre—the truth or falsehood of our utterances surely cannot hang on facts like this.

Moore has a response that he could make to this: he maintains that in mixed contexts more than one proposition may be expressed. If the speaker is enlightened and focusing on aspects, but the audience is not, an aspect-sensitive proposition will be expressed with respect to the speaker's context and an aspect-insensitive proposition with respect to the audience's. These propositions may well differ in truth value. In some cases, then, the speaker will express a true proposition relative to their own context and a false one relative to the audience's. This is what Moore would take to happen in Edna and Frieda's conversation—Edna's utterance would be true relative to her own context but false relative to Frieda's. Presumably, Moore would take there to be multiple audience contexts in the auditorium case: Edna might express a true proposition relative to her own context, the same true proposition relative to the context of the enlightened audience, and a false proposition relative to the context of the single unenlightened audience member.

I don't find this a very satisfying or natural response, although it is a possible one. The question, 'Was Edna's utterance true?' does not seem to be one whose answer should change depending on whether one member of the audience is called away at a crucial moment. Yet Moore must insist that the answer does change: if the unenlightened audience member is absent, we can give a simply answer of 'yes'; if not, we must answer 'yes for Edna and 4999 audience members, no for the other'. Moreover, suppose we now enlighten the one unenlightened audience member. It does not seem to me that this person would accept that Edna's utterance had been false for her—she would insist that the utterance had been true. Moore's response, then, is seriously in conflict with our intuitions about the truth values of simple sentences. Since his goal, like Forbes's, is to accommodate these intuitions, this seems to me an important problem.

We have seen that one sort of problem—too much speaker control—arises for accounts that leave aspect-sensitivity entirely up to the speaker. Another sort of problem—too much audience control—arises for those that share responsibility for aspect sensitivity between the speaker and the audience. These problems alone are serious enough, particularly when considered together. However, what is even more serious is a problem that arises for either approach (and, we will see, for many others). This problem, the Enlightenment Problem, is considered in the next section.

2.2.3.3 *The Enlightenment Problem*[16]

All of the versions of Moore's and Forbes's context-dependent views on the semantics of simple sentences are committed to the idea that this contextual variation is determined in part by the enlightenment of speakers and audiences. Other factors—like their interests and intentions—also play a role; and the versions vary as to *whose* enlightenment they take to be relevant. But neither theorist has any doubt that the enlightenment of conversational participants is relevant. Unless at least the speaker is enlightened (and possibly the audience as well) no aspect-sensitive proposition can be expressed. I will suggest, however, that this basic commitment is fundamentally misguided: a view that is committed to this necessary condition cannot capture our intuitions about simple sentences. The reason for this is that our intuitions simply aren't affected by conversational participants' degrees of enlightenment in the required way. This shows that it is wrong to posit a contextual variation that hinges on conversational participants' degrees of enlightenment. Whatever fuels our contextually varying intuitions, it can't be that.

Consider again sentence (1), which seemed true:

(1) Superman leaps more tall buildings than Clark Kent does.

This sentence cannot be true, according to Moore and Forbes, unless it is uttered in an enlightened context. This cannot occur unless the speaker at least is enlightened, and—for Moore, and possibly Forbes also—the audience must be enlightened too. But when you read (1), and thought it was true, you didn't give any thought to the question of what sort of context you should be considering it in—you didn't wonder whether the audience, or even the speaker, knew of Superman's

---

[16] This objection was originally developed in Braun and Saul (2002).

double life. The fact that you didn't is some reason to suppose that you don't intuitively take these to be relevant to (1)'s truth value.

This is not, however, decisive. The reason you failed to consider whether the speaker was enlightened may well have been that you could safely—and tacitly—assume the speaker to be so. After all, pretty much everyone who discusses the Superman story is enlightened with respect to it. Moreover, you read the sentence in a book on substitution puzzle cases. It would be quite reasonable to neglect the possibility of unenlightened speakers.

But what happens when this possibility is introduced? Suppose I tell you now that you were meant to consider (1) as uttered by Lois, unenlightened, in a conversation with her unenlightened co-worker Miles about why Superman is so much more interesting romantically than that dull Clark. If Moore and Forbes are right, you should now change your mind. 'Ah', you should say to yourself, 'I was assuming that the speaker knew all about the double life. If they don't, their utterance can't be true'. But you don't do this. In fact, most likely you won't even waver over your previous view. Learning that the speaker is unenlightened is simply not the sort of thing that affects your intuitions about the truth values of utterances of simple sentences. But for Forbes and Moore, it is precisely the sort of thing that *must* affect your intuitions—if your intuitions are to be captured by their views.

Interestingly, however, it would be wrong to suppose that *no* information about context can alter your initial intuitions about (1). Indeed, some such information might well have quite a strong effect. Suppose, for example, that I say you were meant to consider (1) as uttered in a conversation between two Naïve Millians whose commitment to their view has convinced them to use the names 'Superman' and 'Clark Kent' fully interchangeably. The speaker uttered (1) as an example of an obviously false claim. Once you have been told this, I suspect you will take your initial intuition to have been mistaken. You will instead maintain that this utterance was false. Alternatively, you may yourself be committed to using the names fully interchangeably—or, at least, interchangeably in simple sentences. When you remind yourself of this view, and keep it in the forefront of your mind, you will not allow that utterance (1) could be true. The contrast between these cases and the Lois/Miles one, it seems to me, is stark. And it shows us that although our intuitions are affected by contextual factors, they are not tracking what Moore and Forbes take them to be tracking.

2.3 PREDELLI

Stefano Predelli has recently offered an account that differs in important ways from those suggested by Moore and Forbes. His account allows for contextual variation in the truth conditions of a simple sentence, but it does so in a very different way. Predelli is a Millian: a name never contributes anything but its referent to the proposition expressed by a sentence containing it. Moreover, the propositions expressed by simple sentences do not vary with context. Nonetheless, Predelli allows for contextual variation in what situations in the world would make such propositions true.

Predelli presents this view by way of an example of his own, (14).

(14) Bruce Wayne wears a mask.

An utterance of (14) will always express a proposition consisting just of the individual Batman/Bruce Wayne and the property of wearing a mask. However, Predelli maintains, the extension of 'wears a mask' will vary with context.[17] This seems fairly sensible: sometimes what matters is just wearing a mask occasionally, under any circumstances; sometimes particular circumstances will matter. In one context, Wayne's doctors—who know all about his double life—might be discussing whether his rash is caused by the mask that he wears at night. In this context, Wayne will count as a mask-wearer, so (14) will be true. In another context, the topic under discussion (again by conversational participants fully aware of Wayne's double life) are concerned with whether he shows up at the boardroom in a mask. In this latter context, Wayne will not count as a mask-wearer, so (14) will be false.

Things get trickier when we turn to our familiar sentence (1):

(1) Superman leaps more tall buildings than Clark Kent.

An utterance of this sentence will express a proposition that contains (a) the pair consisting of Superman/Kent, taken twice and (b) the relation of leaping more tall buildings than. What will vary with context is which states of the world will count as ones in which this relation holds. The relation's extension will sometimes, but only sometimes,

---

[17] For Predelli, context determines (among other things) what point of evaluation is relevant for the truth value of a sentence. This point of evaluation will fix the extensions of predicates.

include the pair that consists of Superman/Clark twice over. According to Predelli, the use of the names 'Superman' and 'Clark Kent' may make the superhero and reporter personae salient. If they do, it is the building-leaping proclivities of these personae (rather than the individuals) that will be compared in order to arrive at a truth value for such an utterance of (1).

This view, it seems to me, faces several problems. First, Predelli makes use of personae but does not tell us what they are. Without further information on this topic, there is no reason to suppose that the Aspect Problem will not arise for Predelli's account as it did for Forbes's and Moore's. Next, Predelli maintains that the feature of context which decides what matters for settling the truth value of a simple sentence utterance is the interests, intentions, and so on of conversational participants. He does not tell us very much about how this works, so there is no reason to suppose that his account will escape the Enlightenment Problem. Most importantly, however, it seems to me that Predelli's account makes a deeply puzzling claim: that the proposition consisting of Superman/Clark twice over and the relation of leaping more tall buildings than may be true. This seems to me just baffling. It does make sense to suppose that what counts as wearing a mask varies, and that Bruce Wayne will qualify in some contexts but not in others. But it does not make sense to suppose that some individual may ever leap more tall buildings than himself. In explaining this idea, Predelli makes reference to variation in what counts as 'evidence' for the claim's truth (2004: 118). Although it seems right that there would indeed be such variation in what counts as evidence, I do not see how this can support a claim of variation in truth value for the proposition at issue. In order to avoid commitment to this claim, however, Predelli would need to either (a) give up the claim that a sentence like (1) may be true or (b) maintain that sentence (1), when it is true, expresses a different proposition. To do the first is to give up the goal of a semantic account that accords with anti-substitution intuitions about (at least some) simple sentences. To do the second is to move to an account much more like those we have already seen from Forbes and Moore. Without quite a bit more explanation, then, his account does not seem like an improvement.[18]

---

[18] The problem noted seems especially problematic given the way that Predelli motivates his view. The chief advantage of his view over its rivals is meant to be that it upholds all of the four plausible theses about semantic theorising. It is not so clear how

2.4 SUMMING UP

In this chapter, we have examined semantic accounts that aim to give results in accord with anti-substitution intuitions about simple sentences. We saw that accounts not incorporating a significant degree of context-dependence fail to capture key intuitions. But accounts incorporating context-dependence encounter problems as well. The two most significant problems, we will see, turn out to arise in various forms for other accounts as well. These are the problems that I have called the Aspect Problem and the Enlightenment Problem:

- *The Aspect Problem:* Any account making use of intuition-matching propositions that include aspects or modes of personification needs to be able to explain what these entities are, how it is that we manage to communicate about them, and what the intuition-matching propositions involving them are. The accounts discussed so far do not meet this challenge.
- *The Enlightenment Problem:* For a context-dependent account, whether or not an aspect-sensitive proposition is expressed hinges in part on the states of enlightenment of conversational participants. In particular, no such proposition can be expressed unless the speaker (and possibly the audience) is enlightened. For an account like this to succeed in capturing our intuitions, these intuitions would have to vary with conversational participants' (or at least speakers') states of enlightenment. But they do not.

This chapter has shown the difficulty of trying to arrive at a semantic theory that yields intuitively correct truth conditions for simple sentence utterances. I have not decisively shown that no such theory is possible. But I hope to have provided a significant degree of motivation to embark on the quest for some alternative approach to simple sentences, one that explains why our intuitions about these sentences may go wrong. The rest of this book will be devoted, in one way or another, to the search for a satisfying explanation of this form. It will assume that our anti-substitution intuitions about simple sentences are in error, and it will attempt to explain these errors. That is, it will assume that the

much of an advantage this is if it comes at the price of allowing the truth of a proposition consisting of a, a, and the property of leaping more tall buildings than. Surely another highly plausible thesis is that any such proposition must be false.

names at issue in the current puzzle cases are co-referential, and that substitution of co-referential names always succeeds in the absence of what are standardly taken to be opacity-producing constructions. (I take no position here on whether such substitution must succeed in the presence of such constructions as well, though I do discuss this issue in Appendix B.) As these efforts proceed, we will see just how intractable the problems posed by simple sentences are. We will eventually find a way to avoid these problems, but it will necessitate a non-traditional approach to truth-conditional intuitions.

3

Simple Sentences and Implicatures

Those who want to uphold anti-substitution intuitions about simple sentences must offer semantic accounts that yield this result. In the last chapter, we saw many problems for accounts that attempt to do this, especially the Enlightenment Problem and the Aspect Problem. When attempts to uphold intuitions fail, a natural alternative is to claim that the intuitions are in error. As noted in the preface, one who makes this move must explain why the intuitions are in error; as also noted, the most traditional way of doing this is to invoke conversational implicatures. (We saw an extended example of this with the discussion of Naïve Implicature Theory in Chapter 1.) In this chapter we will explore this most traditional of options for explaining away truth-conditional intuitions[1] about simple sentences. I examine Alex Barber's account, but I also look at a variety of possible alternative accounts, including ones based on non-standard understandings of 'conversational implicature'. In the end, we will see that the Enlightenment Problem and the Aspect Problem (in slightly different versions) arise for implicature-based attempts to accommodate simple sentence intuitions. These continuing problems serve to motivate the next two chapters' search for the assumptions that give rise to these problems and ways of avoiding them.

3.1 BARBER'S ACCOUNT

Alex Barber (2000) offers an account of simple sentences on which anti-substitution intuitions turn out to be mistaken. He explains away these intuitions by invoking conversational implicatures. But he also

---

[1] Reminder: I use the phrase 'truth conditions' to refer to the truth values of a sentence in a context, evaluated both at the actual world and at other possible worlds. Truth-conditional intuitions are intuitions about these truth values.

wishes to insist that we need an account of belief reporting that
vindicates anti-substitution intuitions. As I have argued, this means
that he needs to tell a story explaining why it is acceptable to explain
away simple sentences intuitions but unacceptable to explain away
belief reporting intuitions. Barber does this, we will see, by arguing
that his implicature-based account of simple sentences is unavailable to
those who do not allow substitution to be blocked in belief reporting
sentences.

3.1.1 The account

According to Alex Barber's proposal, 'Superman' and 'Clark Kent' make
different contributions to the propositions expressed by utterances
of sentences containing them. Nonetheless, simple sentences that differ
only in the substitution of co-referential names must have the same truth
value. In non-simple sentences like belief reports, such substitution *can*
make a difference to truth value.

As we saw in Chapter 1, substitution failures in unenlightened
contexts are relatively easy to account for. This is true on Barber's
account as well—although, as we will see, he argues that such contexts
are especially problematic for Naïve Millians. Such substitution failures
can be explained, he maintains, by the fact that, for those who do not
realise that 'Superman' and 'Clark Kent' co-refer, sentences like (1) and
(1*), or (2) and (2*), will have different cognitive significance.[2]

(1) Clark Kent went into the phone booth, and Superman came out.
(1*) Superman went into the phone booth, and Clark Kent came out.
(2) Superman leaps more tall buildings than Clark Kent.
(2*) Superman leaps more tall buildings than Superman.

Barber does not go into detail on this point, but it seems clear that he
takes utterances of (1) and (1*), and (2) and (2*), to express different propositions. One who encounters and understands an utterance of (1) will
grasp one proposition, and one who encounters and understands an
utterance of (1*) will grasp another proposition. Unenlightened people
who encounter (1) and (1*) will not be in a position to realise that these
propositions must have the same truth value. Indeed, they are quite likely
to think that they differ in truth value. Barber writes, 'we can express

---

[2] This explanation mirrors the traditional Fregean explanation of such intuitions
discussed in Chapter 1.

this by distinguishing between a *difference in the cognitive significance to a person* of a pair of sentences of their language, and a *difference in the truth-conditions* of that same pair' (Barber 2000: 302, his emphasis).

This approach alone cannot make sense of the anti-substitution intuitions of enlightened speakers. Enlightened speakers know that 'Superman' and 'Clark Kent' name the same person, so 'ignorance of the identity is no longer available to generate a dissociation between sameness in cognitive significance for the [conversational] participants and sameness in truth-conditions' (Barber 2000: 302). Barber suggests, however, that a pragmatic explanation is readily available, one utilising Gricean conversational implicatures.

To see how this works, assume that we are trying to explain how it is that an utterance of (2) by one enlightened speaker to another might seem true. For Barber, this will be because the false utterance of (2) carries a true implicature, roughly captured by (2B).

(2) Superman leaps more tall buildings than Clark Kent.
(2B) Superman/Clark, when Supermanising, leaps more tall buildings than Superman/Clark, when Clark Kentising.

We will discuss Supermanising and Clark Kentising in more detail shortly. For the moment, however, let's work with Barber's simplest characterisation: Superman is Supermanising when he is appearing as Superman (2000: 304). In support of his implicature acount, Barber notes that his suggested implicature is *calculable*. As we saw in Chapter 1, one necessary condition for implicating that *P* by saying that *Q* is that it be possible for the audience to work out the implicature on the basis of the assumption that the speaker is being cooperative. Barber claims that the enlightened audience would be able to work out the implicature (2B) from the utterance of (2), by reasoning roughly as follows:

She (the speaker) just said that Superman leaps more tall buildings than Clark Kent. But that can't be true, because Superman just is Clark Kent, and she knows this. However, I know she's trying to be cooperative and say true things. So she must be trying to get something else across—she must be trying to convey to me that the sorts of conditions obtain which would prompt an unenlightened person to utter (2). That is, she must be trying to tell me that Superman leaps more tall buildings when he's *Supermanising* than when he's *Clark Kentising*.[3]

---

[3] This is my reconstruction not Barber's. However, the differences are not significant. See Barber (2000: 303–4).

Thus an utterance of (2) among the enlightened will generally carry the implicature (2B). As a result, it will seem appropriate and even be judged to be true. An utterance of (2*), however, will carry no such implicature—since 'Superman' occurs on both sides of 'leaps more tall buildings than'. It will, then, be infelicitous, and it will seem clearly false. This is why speakers will be resistant to the substitution taking us from (2) to (2*). Barber describes the situation this way: 'substitution failure is possible at the pragmatic level, at the level of what is conveyed or implicated' even when substitution succeeds 'at the semantic level' (2000: 303).

Barber maintains that his account offers an extremely natural way to accommodate the anti-substitution intuitions of both the enlightened and the unenlightened. Moreover, he insists that no account like his is available to Naïve Millians. His reason, in broadest outline, is that his account *depends* on maintaining that substitution fails in belief contexts. More specifically, he argues that a Naïve Implicature account cannot explain the anti-substitution intuitions of the unenlightened. The reason for this, he claims, is that on such an account there is no room for a difference in cognitive significance between sentences like (1) and (1*) or (2) and (2*). According to Barber, 'sentences S1 and S2 differ in cognitive significance for A iff A does not believe S1 and S2 to have identical truth conditions' (p. 302). In order for substitution of co-referential names like 'Superman' and 'Clark Kent' to make a difference to cognitive significance (in this case, to Lois), Barber insists (pp. 306–7), it must be that (3) is true while (3*) is false:

(3) Lois believes that Superman is the semantic value of 'Superman'.
(3*) Lois believes that Clark is the semantic value of 'Superman'.[4]

Salmon and Soames do not allow for the possibility of (3) and (3*) differing in truth value, while a Fregean account like Barber's does. Thus, Barber claims, Salmon and Soames's account cannot permit a difference in cognitive significance in simple sentences that differ only in the substitution of co-referential names. Barber notes that Salmon and Soames's account makes use of guises under which we believe propositions—a person might believe a proposition under one guise while believing its negation under another. Barber claims, though, that

---

[4] One worry about this that I won't pursue here is that it seems committed to the implausible claim that Lois has beliefs about semantic value.

this cannot help Salmon and Soames with the problem he has posed, as (3) and (3*) still cannot differ in truth value.

Barber, then, offers a full reply to the challenge simple sentences pose to opponents of Salmon and Soames's approach. If he is successful, then he has explained both why we may wrongly take simple sentences to differ in truth value, and why it is acceptable to explain away intuitions about simple sentences while insisting that those regarding belief reports must be upheld. According to Barber, *upholding* anti-substitution intuitions about belief reports is essential to *explaining away* anti-substitution intuitions about simple sentences.

3.1.2 Can this approach succeed?

Before tackling Barber's argument that Naïve Millians cannot use implicatures to explain simple sentence intuitions, we need to examine how well Barber's story succeeds at accommodating these intuitions. I will argue that it does not succeed. This is because it faces versions of the Aspect Problem and the Enlightenment Problem:

- *The Aspect Problem:* Barber needs to tell us a convincing story of what attributes like Supermanising and Kentising are. This story needs to tell us how these things are picked out, and how we manage to communicate about them. I argue that his account does not do this.
- *The Enlightenment Problem:* It will turn out that Barber's account can only explain our truth-conditional intuitions if these intuitions vary (in the right way) with the conversational participants' states of enlightenment. Since they do not, his account fails to explain our intuitions.

3.1.2.1 The Aspect Problem

The Aspect Problem, applied to Barber's account, is that of giving a satisfying account of attributes like Supermanising and Clark Kentising, combined with a story of how we manage to communicate about these things.

Barber writes that the attributes of Supermanising and Clark Kentising are 'the attributes of appearing such that an actual or imagined ignoramus would refer to one as "Superman" or "Clark Kent" respectively' (p. 304). ('Ignoramus' is Barber's term for an unenlightened person.) But which actual or imagined ignoramus? For Barber, this will vary with context. So, for example, 'when lying de-suited in bed with Lois after having seduced her with his superhuman charms' (p. 306) he is Supermanising because *Lois*—the person actually observing him—would refer to him as 'Superman'. But when he is all alone, in his suit and tie, he is Clark Kentising because a counterfactual normal observer would call him 'Clark Kent'. (Note that the counterfactual normal observer might have no idea whether to call the man in bed with Lois 'Superman' or 'Clark Kent'.) So Superman is Supermanising when unenlightened *others*—which others will vary with context—would call him 'Superman'.[5]

This additional bit of contextual variation does not seem to me to solve the problems that faced aspects and modes of personification. In fact, the contextual variation Barber invokes may even make matters more difficult. At the very least, they introduce a new complication. To see this, let's consider in more detail one of the examples alluded to above. In particular, consider an utterance of (4):

(4) Lois woke up in bed next to Superman but she never woke up next to Clark.

Intuitively, (4) might be true, even though (4*) clearly couldn't be:

(4*) Lois woke up in bed next to Clark, but she never woke up next to Clark.

Barber would claim that (4) and (4*) are both false, and that our intuition that (4) is true is due to the fact that it implicates (4B), which is true.

(4B) Lois woke up in bed next to Superman, when Supermanising, but she never woke up next to Clark, when Clarkising.

In order for this explanation to work, (4B) must of course be true. To evaluate (4B)'s truth, we need to know whether, when Lois woke up next to him, Superman was Supermanising. Barber would say that he was, despite the fact that he was not dressed as Superman, and he was not—let us stipulate—using any of his superpowers. For Barber, this is because *Lois* would call him 'Superman', even though other observers would not. But why should Lois be the one that counts?

One answer might be that if there is an actual observer, that observer is always the one whose opinion settles the matter. But this won't do, as we can see from a slight addition to our story: imagine that Myrtle was spying on Lois through the window as she woke up, and that Myrtle

---

[5] For more on the examples that motivate this sort of contextual variation in Supermanizing, see Saul (1997*b*); Barber (2000).

was shocked to find Lois in bed with a man that she (Myrtle) would call 'Clark'. Now there are two actual observers, who would give different verdicts. If we took the view that the actual observer(s), if any, are always the relevant ones, then (4B) could not be true in the situation described. (It is not clear what truth value it would have. It might lack a truth value; it might have an indeterminate truth value; but it could not simply be true.) But the addition of Myrtle peeping through the window does nothing to alter the intuition that (4) is true—an intuition that Barber would not be able to explain on the proposed version of his account.

A more promising answer might look to the conversational participants to settle which observers count in each given context. But how would this go? For conversational participants to do this, they would seemingly need to be thinking about possible and actual observers of the situations described. This seems very implausible—they will rarely be thinking about any such thing. Perhaps one could argue instead for a dispositional solution—what matters is which observers they would choose if pressed to do so. This is certainly more psychologically realistic. But problems remain. Suppose that (4) is uttered by Dawn to Caleb. Dawn, like Barber, would take Lois's observations to be the ones that count. Caleb, raised as a fundamentalist Christian, was taught (and deeply believes) that the Superman persona was a wholly celibate one. Caleb, then, would be adamant that (4) is false. His certainty in this matter would surely affect his choice of which observers count. As a result, Caleb would insist that the observer who counts is Myrtle.

What happens in the case of such a disagreement? Barber does not consider mixed contexts, so he does not give us guidance on this. One answer is that the implicature is not a full proposition, because no content for 'Supermanising' can be determined in a context where conversational participants disagree over which observers are relevant. The result of this would be a lack of truth value for (4B). But the intuition that (4) is true is completely unaffected by Caleb's strange belief. This intuition still needs explaining, and (4B) cannot be used to explain it on this proposal. Another answer would be that the implicature is indeterminate between two propositions—the one Dawn would choose and the one Caleb would choose. But these propositions have different truth values. So, once more, (4B) fails to be true—and the intuition that (4) is true goes unexplained.

It is hard to see how the contextually-shifting relevant observers can be picked out in a non-question-begging way. ('The ones who get it right' clearly won't do!) Perhaps some satisfying story can be told about how this is done, but we don't yet have it. In the absence of such a story, Barber sill faces the Aspect Problem: we lack a satisfying story about what Supermanising and Clarkising are, and how we communicate about them.

3.1.2.2 Implicature and enlightenment

The Enlightenment Problem arises for Barber because his only mechanism for accommodating the anti-substitution intuitions of the enlightened is conversational implicature. This mechanism proves to be inadequate: there are anti-substitution intuitions from enlightened people that simply cannot be the result of conversational implicatures.

We have already seen that our intuitions about simple sentences do not seem to vary with the states of enlightenment of the conversational participants. The key example showing this involved Lois uttering (2) to her friend Miles.

(2) Superman leaps more tall buildings than Clark.

The intuition that (2) is true, I suggested, does not depend upon whether we take Lois and Miles to be enlightened. This intuition's persistence can no more be explained on Barber's account than on Forbes's or Moore's.

One way to see this problem is to look at Grice's three necessary conditions for conversational implicature.[6] Grice claims that a person conversationally implicates that q by saying that p only if:

(1) he is to be presumed to be following the conversational maxims, or at least the Cooperative Principle;
(2) the supposition that he is aware that, or thinks that, q is required to make his saying or making as if to say p (or doing so in *those* terms) consistent with this presumption; and
(3) the speaker thinks (and would expect the hearer to think that the speaker thinks) that it is within the competence of the hearer to work out, or grasp intuitively, that the supposition mentioned in (2) is required. (Grice 1989: 30–1)

Now recall what Barber takes (2) to implicate, as a way of accounting for the intuitions of the enlightened:

(2B) Superman/Clark when *Supermanising*, leaps more tall buildings than Superman/Clark, when *Clark Kentising*.

---

[6] I discuss my interpretation of these conditions as necessary conditions in Chapter 1, footnote 9.

In order to explain our enlightened intuition that (2) is true in Lois and Miles's conversation, even if Lois and Miles are unenlightened, Barber needs to maintain that (2B) is implicated by Lois's utterance of (2). But neither condition (2) nor condition (3) of Grice's necessary conditions seems to be met. For condition (3) to be met, Lois would have to think that Miles could work out that he must assume her to believe (2B). An unenlightened speaker like Lois would have no reason at all to even entertain this proposition, which involves Supermanising and Clark Kentising. (As we have seen, only enlightened speakers have reason to entertain propositions like these.) She would not, then, think that Miles could work out that he needs to assume her to believe this. For condition (2) Miles's continued presumption of Lois's cooperativeness would need to depend upon him assuming that Lois believes (2B). But this is by no means the case. Miles is unenlightened, so Lois's utterance seems perfectly cooperative—there is no need whatsoever to search around for some belief that can be attributed to her so as to preserve the assumption that she is being cooperative. (2B), then, cannot be implicated by Lois's utterance to Miles. Yet nonetheless we have the intuition that (2) is true. Barber's account seems to have no way to explain this.[7]

A slightly different way to see this is to focus just on Grice's calculability requirement—in order for Lois to implicate that (2B), Miles has to be able to work out from Lois's utterance that she believes that (2B). But Miles is in no position to do this. Since he thinks that 'Superman' and 'Clark Kent' refer to different individuals, there is nothing to suggest to him that Lois is thinking of one individual who both Supermanises and Clark Kentises. Lois's utterance, then, cannot implicate (2B). There is, then, no true implicated proposition available to explain our intuition that (2) is true.

One response to this might be to suggest that implicatures like (2B) are always carried. Perhaps, for example, for any utterances of a sentence of the form (5)—where N is a name, audiences always grasp a proposition of the form (5B) as a part of their interpretation, and speakers always think that they will do so.

(5) N is F.
(5B) N, when N-ising, is F.

---

[7] Some readers may worry that this response hinges on adhering very closely to Grice's understanding of implicature, and that it is inadequate to address the possibility of accounts based on other understandings of implicatures. They should rest assured that these other understandings will be discussed, both in this chapter and the next.

(And similarly, for other sentence structures involving names.) If this is the case, then there is no difficulty in explaining how (2B) might be implicated in an unenlightened context in which cooperation is assumed (thus meeting Condition (1)). Grice's second condition will also be met because the audience takes it that the speaker must believe (2B)—otherwise his utterance, which all expect to convey (2B), would be highly uncooperative. Condition (3) is met because the speaker expects all this to be worked out. So we now have an explanation of the intuition that (2) is true, even when it is uttered in an unenlightened context.

But it just isn't plausible to suppose that we do always mean things of the form (5B) when we utter sentences of the form (5)—or that we interpret others as doing so. To see this, first recall that some of us are enlightened. And, despite being enlightened, we sometimes mean to talk just about the individuals, and not about their aspects. Consider, for example, an enlightened speaker uttering (6) to another enlightened speaker:

(6) Clark put on his cape and rescued a Nobel prize-winning scientist tied to the trolley tracks last night.

Clearly, this speaker intends to talk simply about the individual, and this is how they will be understood. Nothing about Clark-ising is implicated by this utterance of (6). This is because we only *sometimes* mean or understand claims involving names to convey aspect-sensitive propositions.

Is it plausible to suppose that the *un*enlightened always mean or understand claims involving names as conveying something about aspects—even if the enlightened don't? I don't think it is. First note that we'd need to assume that this happens with every name—not just with names for those who lead double lives—since the unenlightened know nothing of the double lives. This seems to me unlikely. More importantly, however, it's very strange indeed to suppose that it is only once we become enlightened that we manage to utter sentences involving names without meaning something about aspects. If we never become enlightened, we never gain this ability. Now recall that most people don't live double lives. There is no room for us to become enlightened about most people, since there is nothing to be enlightened about. This means that when we are discussing that vast majority of people we are completely unable to do so without meaning something about aspects—no matter how hard we try. And this seems utterly implausible. It doesn't make sense, then, to suppose that implicatures of the form (5B) are always carried by utterances of sentences like (5)—either by all of us, or by the unenlightened.

3.2 NAÏVE IMPLICATURE ACCOUNTS OF SIMPLE SENTENCES

Naïve Millians, of course, may also invoke implicatures in an attempt to explain away our intuitions about simple sentences. It is time now to examine the prospects for such a view—to see if Barber's objection to such an approach succeeds, and to see if it faces other difficulties.

Here I will offer an implicature account on behalf of Naïve Implicature theorists like Salmon and Soames. We will see that it is not vulnerable to Barber's objection. However, I will then show that this account is just as vulnerable as Barber's to the Aspect Problem and the Enlightenment Problem.

3.2.1 A Naïve Implicature account of simple sentences

Salmon and Soames maintain, as we have seen, that a name's sole semantic contribution is always simply its referent. Co-referential names may always be substituted for one another without any change in proposition expressed or in truth value. Belief reports like (7) and (7*), below, then, must take the same truth conditions. All that these reports do, semantically speaking, is attribute belief in the same proposition to the same speaker.

(7) Lois believes that Superman flies.
(7*) Lois believes that Clark flies.

However, such belief reports may carry differing conversational impli-catures that can help to explain the intuition that (7) and (7*) may differ in truth value. These implicatures will make reference to the *guises* under which Lois's beliefs are held—an utterance of (7) will very likely implicate that her belief is held under a guise something like 'Superman can fly'; and an utterance of (7*) will very likely implicate that her belief is held under a guise something like 'Clark can fly'. The fact that (7) typically implicates something true and (7*) typically implicates something false can, on this view, explain the intuition that (7) is true and (7*) false.

These guises can also explain the anti-substitution intuitions of the unenlightened about simple sentences. Sentences like (2) and (2*) will present the same proposition under different guises.

(2) Superman leaps more tall buildings than Clark Kent.
(2*) Superman leaps more tall buildings than Superman.

Although these sentences express the same proposition, one who grasps this proposition does so only via the mediation of guises. A person who is unaware that 'Superman' and 'Clark' co-refer may well falsely take sentences (2) and (2*) to differ in truth value. There will be no reason for such a person to doubt that this makes sense. The guises already invoked by the Naïve Implicature account, then, do all the work needed for the intuitions of the unenlightened.

More work, however, is needed to account for the intuitions of the enlightened. After all, such people know that 'Superman' and 'Clark Kent' co-refer. They should, then, realise that (2) doesn't make sense—the substitution inference that would get them to (2*) should be fairly obvious. The mere fact that (2) and (2*) present the proposition they express under different guises, then, is not a sufficient explanation. It is natural for the Naïve Implicature theorist to use implicatures to account for the intuitions of the enlightened—just as she did in the case of belief reports. But these implicatures cannot be ones about guises—(2) and (2*) don't concern anyone's states of mind, so implicatures about guises would be very unlikely to arise.

It seems likely that the would-be implicature theorist will have to make roughly the same move that others have done—they will need to invoke something like modes of presentation or aspects. For convenience, let's assume they do this in just the way Barber does. Such a theorist, then, will claim that an utterance of (2) typically conversationally implicates something like what is expressed by (2B).

(2) Superman leaps more tall buildings than Clark Kent.
(2B) Superman/Clark, when Supermanising, leaps more tall buildings than Superman/Clark, when Clark Kentising.

3.2.2 Answering Barber's objection

Barber argues that an account like Salmon and Soames's cannot explain the anti-substitution intuitions of the unenlightened. The reason for this, he claims, is that on such an account there is no room for a difference in cognitive significance between sentences like (1) and (1*) or (2) and (2*). To make room for such a difference, there would have to be a difference in truth value between (3) and (3*):

(3) Lois believes that Superman is the semantic value of 'Superman'.
(3*) Lois believes that Clark is the semantic value of 'Superman'.

Salmon and Soames do not allow for the possibility of (3) and (3*) differing in truth value, while Barber's does. Barber takes a difference in truth value between (3) and (3*) to be essential to an implicature-based account of anti-substitution intuitions about (2) and (2*).

(2) Superman leaps more tall buildings than Clark.
(2*) Superman leaps more tall buildings than Superman.

This is because he takes it that there cannot be a difference in cognitive significance between (2) and (2*) unless there is a difference in truth value between (3) and (3*).

This objection, it seems to me, does not succeed. The reason is that Barber is wrong to claim that Salmon and Soames cannot allow for a difference in cognitive significance for pairs of sentences like (2) and (2*). They do allow for such a difference, making sense of the difference in a way that does not require different truth values for (3) and (3*).[8] Consider again Barber's own definition of cognitive significance: 'sentences S1 and S2 differ in cognitive significance for A iff A does not believe S1 and S2 to have identical truth conditions'. Now consider what Salmon and Soames would say about sentences (2) and (2*). Salmon and Soames would claim that sentences (2) and (2*) present the very same proposition under different guises (the simplest version of this story would be one on which these guises are sentences (2) and (2*) themselves). Next, they would say that an unenlightened speaker, presented with the pairs (2) and (2*), would fail to realise that these sentences express the same proposition—because she fails to realise that 'Superman' and 'Clark Kent' name the same individual. The reason she fails to realise this is that the proposition is being presented to her under different guises. As a result, she might well take (2) to be true while (2*) is false. This speaker clearly does not believe (2) and (2*) to have identical truth conditions. Salmon and Soames would say precisely parallel things about the pair (1) and (1*). They are, then, able to recognise a difference in cognitive significance.[9]

Salmon and Soames's account of the difference in cognitive significance between sentences like (2) and (2*) in no way depends upon a

---

[8] This is actually a point in favour of their theory, since Lois is quite unlikely to have any beliefs at all about semantic values—so both sentences will certainly be false.

[9] It is perhaps worth emphasizing that guises are essential to this response. Millians who do not make use of guises, such as Thau (2002), do not have this response available. For problems facing such views, see Braun (2002).

difference in truth value between (3) and (3*). Their failure to allow for such a difference, then, poses no difficulty for their account. A proponent of Barber's approach, then, is still in need of a reason to accept the violation of anti-substitution intuitions about simple sentences while refusing to accept parallel intuition violations regarding belief sentences.

3.2.3 The real problems with Naïve Implicature explanations of simple sentence intuitions

The real problems with Naïve Implicature explanations of simple sentence intuitions are precisely the ones that plagued Barber's account: We do not have an adequate account of Supermanising and Clark Kentising that can overcome the Aspect Problem, and we still have anti-substitution intuitions in cases where there are no implicatures available to explain them (the Enlightenment Problem). The first point should be obvious—our Naïve theorist has added nothing to the account of Supermanising offered by Barber. The second point should also be pretty clear. Learning that Lois and Miles were both unenlightened when Lois uttered (2) has no effect on our intuitions about (2)'s truth value.

(2) Superman leaps more tall buildings than Clark Kent.

But if the speaker isn't enlightened, she cannot implicate anything like (2B).

(2B) Superman/Clark, when *Supermanising,* leaps more tall buildings than Superman/Clark, when *Clark Kentising.*

This account, then—just like Barber's—fails to explain all of the intuitions that it needs to explain.

3.3 ALTERNATIVE VIEWS OF CONVERSATIONAL IMPLICATURE AND THE ENLIGHTENMENT PROBLEM

The Enlightenment Problem for implicature-based explanations of simple sentence intuitions may so far seem to be the result of the particular definition of 'conversational implicature' I have employed—Grice's. But this is not the only understanding of conversational implicature that is possible. So it is natural to wonder whether an implicature account based on a different understanding might succeed where those we have discussed have failed. It turns out, though, that the details of Grice's understanding are not essential to the Enlightenment Problem. Even if we assume an alternative understanding of implicature, an utterance of (2) by an unenlightened person is still unable to implicate what's said by (2B). Below, I show that accounts based on two very different understandings of conversational implicature have this result. In this next chapter, I will show just how general the problem is, and further motivate my concerns.

3.3.1 Sperber and Wilson

Relevance Theorists, like Dan Sperber and Deirdre Wilson (1986, 1995), focus much of their attention on the psychological processes of utterance interpretation. In part as a result of this focus, they have developed a theory on which implicature is a somewhat different notion from that which concerned Grice.[10] Sperber and Wilson do not require that Grice's three necessary conditions be met in order for a conversational implicature to be present. Their definition of 'implicature' is the following: 'Any assumption communicated, but not explicitly, is implicitly communicated: it is an implicature' (1986: 252). It is not entirely clear what this comes to. But it is clear that, for Sperber and Wilson, what is implicated must be a part of the audience's interpretation of an utterance.[11] Indeed, in discussing problems with other accounts both they and their followers frequently invoke the requirement that what is implicated must be psychologically real to the audience.[12] No proposition may be implicated, then, without being grasped by the audience.

This requirement—that implicatures must be grasped by audiences—is sufficient to bring it about that an implicature account based on Relevance Theory will also fail to capture all of our intuitions. To see this, recall the fact that neither the speaker's nor the audience's degree of enlightenment had an impact on the intuition that Lois's utterance of (2) could be true.

---

[10] For more on how I understand the relationship between Relevance Theory and Grice, see Saul (2002*a*).

[11] For a fuller discussion of this aspect of their view, see Saul (2002*a*).

[12] See, for example, Wilson and Sperber (1981); Sperber and Wilson (1986); Carston (1991).

(2) Superman leaps more tall buildings than Clark Kent.

But if the audience is unenlightened, then he can't be grasping (2B) when (2) is uttered.

(2B) Superman/Clark, when *Supermanising,* leaps more tall buildings than Superman/Clark, when *Clark Kentising.*

This means, for Relevance Theorists, that the unenlightened Lois's utterance of (2) to the unenlightened Miles cannot possibly implicate something like (2B).

Carston's most recent version of Relevance Theory (Carston 2002) only deepens this problem. On this version, it is clear that the focus is not just on the audience's state of mind but also on the speaker's. Conversational implicatures must not only be grasped by audiences but also meant by speakers (2002: 19). This additional requirement only makes things worse for an implicature-based proposal. As we have seen, the unenlightened Lois has no reason to entertain, let alone mean, (2B). (2B), then, is doubly ruled out as an implicature—both by Miles's inability to grasp it and by Lois's inability to mean it. Moving to a Relevance-Theoretic notion of implicature, then, will do nothing to help the defender of an implicature account of simple sentence intuitions.[13]

3.3.2 Davis

Wayne Davis has a very different view of implicature. For him, implicature is a matter of speaker meaning and not one of audience interpretation. According to Davis, what a speaker implicates is what she means to convey by saying something else (Davis 1998: 5). Whether the audience picks up on the implicature—or is even able to pick up on the implicature—is of no importance. Miles's lack of enlightenment, and consequent inability to work out that the speaker thinks (2B) does not prevent (2B) from being implicated.

(2B) Superman/Clark, when *Supermanising,* leaps more tall buildings than Superman/Clark, when *Clark Kentising.*

---

[13] It is worth noting that Relevance Theorists would be very unlikely to be sympathetic to any such use of their account. In general, they oppose the idea of using implicatures to explain away intuitions, using their psychological reality requirement to argue against its tenability.

Nonetheless, Davis's version of implicature is not one that will save Barber's account: Davis requires the speaker to mean the implicated proposition, and we have already seen that an unenlightened Lois will not mean to convey (2B). (2B), then, is not implicated. The intuition that Lois's utterance is false, then, has no explanation on this account.

We have by no means canvassed all theories of implicature—there are many such theories, and they differ in important details. However, what is emerging is that (2B) is a very unlikely candidate for implicature in Lois and Miles's conversation: neither the speaker nor the audience is in any position to grasp it. Neither would intend it or make it part of their interpretation of the other's utterance. More generally, the situation is this: conversational participants will have no reason to think in terms of aspects, modes of personification, and the like unless they are enlightened with respect to the relevant double-life. For an implicature view, explaining the problematic intuitions—that an utterance of (2) is true, or that (1) and (1*) may differ in truth value—requires postulating aspect-sensitive implicated propositions. But if conversational participants are unenlightened, they will have no reason to even consider such propositions. And the effect of this is that such propositions simply cannot be implicated: there are no theories on which a proposition that neither the speaker nor the audience is even in a position to grasp may count as an implicature. An implicature view, then, cannot explain our anti-substitution intuitions about conversations between the unenlightened.

3.4 SUMMING UP

In this chapter, we have seen that implicature-based explanations of our simple sentence intuitions suffer from problems quite similar to those that arise for context-dependent semantic accounts of these intuitions. The Aspect Problem is not solved by putting reference to aspects or modes of personification into implicatures rather than semantic content—we still need to know what these are and how we communicate about them, and we still lack an adequate explanation. And a version of the Enlightenment Problem plagues implicature views as well—our intuitions still do not track conversational participants' states of enlightenment in the required ways.

In the next chapter, I turn to the task of diagnosis: why are the accounts of simple sentence intuitions in the literature so prone to these problems? What assumptions are being made, and why? This will lay the groundwork for the task of Chapters 5 and 6: finding a new way of dealing with truth-conditional intuitions.

4

The Enlightenment Problem
and a Common Assumption

The most promising attempts to accommodate our simple sentence intuitions—those incorporating substantial context-dependence—have
faced two major problems: the Enlightenment Problem and the Aspect Problem. In this chapter and the next my focus will be on the
Enlightenment Problem. The current chapter will be largely concerned
with diagnosis—a diagnosis that will ultimately serve to motivate a new
approach to truth-conditional intuitions.[1] I will begin by identifying a
common tacit assumption, which I call 'Expressed or Implicated' (EOI),
that seems to play an important role in producing the Enlightenment
Problem. Next I will explore reasons that theorists may have been
inclined to assume (EOI), arguing that these reasons do not in fact
support (EOI). Finally, I will take a brief look at some psychological
results that help us to see the implausibility of (EOI).

4.1 IDENTIFYING AN ASSUMPTION

The accounts that have fared best in accounting for our truth-conditional intuitions about simple sentences have been those that made
use of contextual variation to do so. Thus far, these have come in
two broad varieties. The first variety postulates that our intuitions
are correct: they arise from successfully grasping and correctly evaluating the propositions expressed by utterances of simple sentences, which
have just the truth conditions we intuitively take them to have. The
second variety claims that our intuitions are incorrect, because they

[1] Reminder: I use the phrase 'truth conditions' to refer to the truth values of a
sentence in a context, evaluated both at the actual world and at other possible worlds.
Truth-conditional intuitions are intuitions about these truth values.

are due not to what is expressed by utterances of simple sentences, but to what these utterances implicate. On this sort of story, although utterances of simple sentences do not have the truth conditions we take them to have, they carry implicatures whose truth conditions do match the ones that we intuitively assign. Both varieties, then, make use of propositions whose truth conditions match those that we intuitively assign to utterances of simple sentences. For one sort of account, such propositions are expressed, while for the other sort of account they are implicated. But the role of such propositions in both cases is similar: it is responsible for our truth-conditional intuitions, which are due to correctly grasping and evaluating such propositions.

This common role leads to a common problem. The expressed or implicated proposition that is meant to match our intuitions turns out not to in certain key cases. And this problem arises due to common features of the two sorts of accounts. For the semantic accounts, broadly speaking, the conversational participants' states of mind are crucial to determining what is *expressed*.[2] However, our intuitions do not vary with conversational participants' states of mind in the required way. For the pragmatic accounts, the conversational participants' states of mind are crucial to determining what is *implicated*. Again, though, our intuitions do not vary with the conversational participants' states of mind in the needed way. As a result, there are cases in which it is impossible to find a proposition, expressed or implicated, whose truth conditions match those indicated by our intuitions.

This suggests, it seems to me, that it is time to examine a methodological assumption that has thus far been kept in the background: that intuitions are to be explained by postulating propositions, expressed or implicated, whose truth conditions match those that we intuitively assign to utterances of simple sentences. Call this assumption *Expressed or Implicated (EOI)*.

Expressed or Implicated (EOI): For an utterance of a sentence S in a context C, the truth-conditional intuitions of competent, rational speakers who are

---

[2] The claim in the text above is a slight oversimplification: on Predelli's (2004) account, as we saw in Chapter 1, the conversational participants' most important role is in determining the truth conditions of what is expressed—rather than what is expressed itself. What is expressed by utterances of simple sentences does not, for Predelli, vary in the ways that Moore and Forbes take it to. However, the variation in truth conditions is determined in just the way that it is for Moore and Forbes.

relevantly well-informed must match the truth conditions of either what is (semantically) expressed or what is implicated by S in C.[3]

Although theorists do not explicitly commit themselves to (EOI), the literature on simple sentences that we have surveyed so far[4] has proceeded *as though* theorists accepted a principle like (EOI). In particular, they offer only accounts that accord with it. This restricted diet of options would make sense if theorists had some good reason to assume the truth of a principle like (EOI). It seems to me, however, that they do not. And that is what I will be arguing in this chapter.

A note regarding (EOI): (EOI) concerns the intuitions of the rational and relevantly well-informed.[5] The reason for this is that the intuitions of the irrational and ill-informed are an obviously poor guide to the matters that concern us—they make errors which are due simply to misinformation and irrationality. This restriction fits well with the discussion thus far of simple sentences: theorists have only attempted to find intuition-matching propositions for the intuitions of the (rational, well-informed) enlightened; the intuitions of the unenlightened can be otherwise explained.

This chapter is concerned with (EOI), an important methodological principle that I take to have had an impact on discussions of simple sentences (as well as other matters). As a result, much of the discussion will not be *directly* concerned with simple sentences. Nonetheless, its relationship to simple sentences will (I hope) be clear.

One who accepts (EOI) will take it that their only options for accommodating truth-conditional intuitions involve either implicated or expressed propositions. This restricted focus makes sense on the assumption that the only way our intuitions might go astray is by tracking implicatures rather than what is expressed. But why might one assume this? In the next sections, I discuss some methodological starting places that might motivate (or seem to motivate) such an assumption.

---

[3] This principle is very similar to the one that Braun and Saul (2002: 14) called the Matching Proposition principle (MP).

[4] The exception to this in the literature is Braun and Saul (2002). The account offered in Chapter 6 is a development of this one.

[5] There are obviously some important terms in need of definition here, in particular 'relevantly well-informed'. We certainly wouldn't want to understand 'relevantly well-informed' in such a way that a speaker counts as relevantly well-informed just in case they are right about the truth conditions of the utterance, for example. This is a difficult matter. I don't have such a definition to offer, but for the purposes of substitution puzzle cases, being relevantly well-informed clearly requires being enlightened. The absence of detail on this matter should not be damaging to my discussion: my reasons for rejecting (EOI) do not at all concern the details of this requirement.

4.2 GRICE AND (EOI)

Invocations of conversational implicature, of course, have their starting place in Grice's work. In Grice's work, however, the relevant contrast was not between *what is semantically expressed* and *what is implicated* but instead between *what is said* and *what is implicated*. For Grice, an utterance of a sentence S says that P iff two conditions are satisfied:

(a) in uttering S, the speaker means that P; and
(b) P corresponds at least very closely to the linguistic meaning of S.[6]

Condition (a) is often overlooked and sometimes explicitly disavowed by Griceans.[7] Condition (b) *suggests* (though it does not explicitly state) that S will say that P only if P is semantically expressed by S. As a result, it is easy (though now increasingly controversial) to equate Grice's *what is said* with what is *semantically expressed*. If we do this, then (EOI) is equivalent to a more Gricean-sounding principle, (SOI):

Said or Implicated (SOI): For an utterance of a sentence S in a context C, the truth-conditional intuitions of competent, rational speakers who are relevantly well-informed must match the truth conditions of either what is said or what is implicated by S in C.

It seems to me that Grice's work on implicature, misunderstood in certain popular ways and combined with certain background assumptions, could lead one to suppose that our truth-conditional intuitions (once we are fully informed of relevant facts) must match either what is said or what is implicated. That is, it could make (SOI) seem quite a natural methodological principle—and this, in turn, may lead one to restrict one's options in a way that accords with (EOI). In what follows, I look at two ways of understanding Grice's theory that could give rise to this line of thought, and I argue that both are mistaken.

4.3 THE SPEAKER MEANING PERSPECTIVE

One very natural thought is that what matters most to us in our use of language is communicating what we mean and figuring out what others

---

[6] This is a loose version of Bach's Syntactic Correlation Constraint, as a loose version is all I need for my purposes. For more on this constraint, see Bach (2001). What is said is not completely determined by sentence meaning, as Grice notes that the referents of indexical terms are relevant to what is said but not determined by sentence meaning.
[7] Bach criticises this aspect of Grice's view in his (2001): 17.

mean. We are interested in what is said mainly because it is a route to discovering what is meant. Because of this, our focus is generally primarily on speaker meaning, and only secondarily (if at all) on what is said. It is this fact that introduces the potential for confusion. When we consider an utterance, we naturally focus on what is meant. This focus of ours leads to mistaken judgments about what is said. When we attempt to reflect on the truth conditions of what is said, we may instead be focusing on what is meant. We may be especially likely to make such an error if the route from what is said to what is meant seems a particularly simple one. If some phrase is very commonly used as a way of meaning something beyond what it strictly speaking says, we are particularly likely to confuse what is meant with what is said. We may even become confused by sentences presented in isolation (that is, even without knowing anything of the context in which they are uttered). If we are aware of what speakers would commonly mean by the sentences, we may well focus on that rather than on what the sentences strictly speaking say.

Now consider another commonly held belief. According to many standard presentations, speaker meaning divides exhaustively into what is said and what is implicated.[8] According to this line of thought, implicature is Grice's way of accommodating those aspects of speaker meaning that do not make it into what is said. If this idea is combined with the idea that our truth-conditional intuitions track speaker meaning, it will be very natural to conclude that our intuitions must be accommodated either by what is said or by what is implicated. When our intuitions go wrong, it is because we are focusing on what the speaker means rather than on what she says—that is, according to this standard line, we are focusing on what she implicates. If all of these thoughts are right, then it may seem natural to suppose that when our intuitions are wrong about what is said, they must be due instead to what is implicated. It may seem natural, then, to suppose that truth-conditional intuitions must match either what is said or what is implicated.

4.3.1 Supporting (SOI)

The considerations above can be brought together to provide an argument that at least seems to provide support for (SOI). I suspect that

---

[8] See, for example, Levinson (1983: 131, 2000: 13); Neale (1990: 73–83, 1992, 2005: 182); Horn (1992: 165).

something like this train of thought is behind the tendency to theorise in accord with (SOI).

First, let's try to bring together the considerations discussed above into an argument. Here is a first attempt at summarising the considerations noted above. (This argument is not intended to be a valid one. Rather, it is a suggestive argument which represents one way of making sense of why theorists might be drawn to a principle like (SOI).)

- Speaker Meaning Tracking (SMT): The truth-conditional intuitions of competent, rational speakers who are fully informed of relevant facts track speaker meaning.
- Speaker Meaning Exhaustiveness (SME): Speaker meaning divides exhaustively into what is said and what is implicated.

These two considerations seem to support the idea that the relevant intuitions must accurately reflect either what is said or what is implicated. That is, they seem to support (SOI).

(SOI): For an utterance of a sentence S in a context C, the truth-conditional intuitions of competent, rational speakers who are relevantly well-informed must match the truth conditions of either what is said or what is implicated by S in C.

(SMT) looks as though it might be true. Certainly it may seem that one who takes our primary communicative interest to be an interest in speaker meaning should accept (SMT). (SME) is widely accepted (as we have already noted). Together, (SMT) and (SME) do seem to provide support for (SOI): If our truth-conditional intuitions track speaker meaning, and speaker meaning divides exhaustively into what is said and what is implicated, then it is natural to suppose that these intuitions should match the truth conditions of either what is said or what is implicated. Below, however, I argue that (SME) is false. Finally, I will argue that even if both (SME) and (SMT) were true, they would not provide good support for (SOI).

4.3.2 Undermining the support for (SOI)—against (SME)

(SME) is false: speaker meaning simply does not divide exhaustively into what is said and what is implicated. To see this, it will help if we briefly review some basics of Grice's theory.

4.3.2.1 *Grice's taxonomy*

4.3.2.1.1 What is said

As we have already seen, what is said, for Grice, is tightly linked to sentence meaning, which he takes to be determined by generalisations about what speakers mean by their utterances of sentences.[9] Grice also requires that what is said be meant by the speaker. If the speaker does not mean that *P*, they do not say that *P*—even if they utter a sentence that conventionally means that *P*.

4.3.2.1.2 Conventional implicatures

Some implicatures are also tightly linked to sentence meaning, indeed determined by it—conventional implicatures. Conventional implicatures are a part of sentence meaning, but not relevant to truth conditions. For Grice, 'Henrietta is English, and therefore brave', carries a conventional implicature that Henrietta's bravery is due to her Englishness. This implicature arises due to the linguistic meaning of 'therefore', and it is therefore uncancellable. However, it is not relevant to the truth value of the utterance: if it turned out that Henrietta's bravery was due not to her Englishness but instead to her early childhood training at an army boot camp, the utterance would still be true.

4.3.2.1.3 Conversational implicatures

As we have already seen, conversational implicatures must satisfy certain conditions. *A* speaker implicates that *q* by saying that *p* only if:

(1) they are to be presumed to be following the conversational maxims, or at least the Cooperative Principle;
(2) the supposition that they are aware that, or think that, *q* is required to make their saying [. . .] *p* (or doing so in *those* terms) consistent with this presumption; and
(3) the speaker thinks (and would expect the hearer to think that the speaker thinks) that it is within the competence of the hearer to work out, or grasp intuitively, that the supposition mentioned in (2) is required. (Grice 1989: 30–1)

In addition, a conversational implicature must be calculable: if *q* is to be implicated, it must be possible for the audience, relying only on the speaker's utterance, background information, and the conversational

---

[9] This view faces serious problems. For an overview of them, see Neale (1992).

maxims, to work out that the speaker intends the audience to believe (or is at least willing to allow the audience to believe) that q (Grice 1989: 31).

Grice's taxonomy, then, includes what is said, what is conventionally implicated, and what is conversationally implicated.[10] Grice's under-standing of each of these notions are sufficient to show that speaker meaning cannot divide exhaustively into what is said and what is im-plicated. I will demonstrate this by offering two examples involving propositions meant by the speaker but neither said nor implicated. The underlying idea behind these examples will be that the speaker may attempt to say or implicate something but fail. Because there is this possibility for failure, there must be room for speaker meaning that is neither said nor implicated—in order to accommodate the propositions that the speaker means but does not succeed in saying or implicating. This means that (SME) is false, since speaker meaning does not divide exhaustively into what is said and what is implicated.[11]

4.3.2.2 *Attempted implicature*

Our first example will be one in which the speaker tries to implicate something but fails. As a result, what she means is neither said nor implicated. (SME) is, then, false.

Speaker Meaning Exhaustiveness (SME): Speaker meaning divides exhaustively into what is said and what is implicated.

I have been asked to write a letter of reference for my very incompetent student Darren. I take Darren to be applying for a philosophy job, and I want to convey that Darren doesn't have much to recommend him as a philosopher. Darren is, however, a fine cook. I write a reference consisting of nothing but the sentence 'Darren is a fabulous cook'. Unbeknownst to me, Darren is actually applying for a job as a trainee chef, having given up on philosophy. Those reading the letter, then, will certainly not take me to be trying to convey that Darren doesn't have much to recommend him as a philosopher. They have no need to assume me to believe anything at all about Darren's philosophical

---

[10] Grice also gestures at the possibility of non-conversational, non-conventional implicatures. He takes these to 'be' like conversational implicatures except that the maxims involved are not the conversational maxims (1989: 28). Because these implicatures are so similar to conversational implicatures, and because the concerns I raise have nothing to do with the exact maxims involved in generating implicatures, I ignore this category here.

[11] I argue for this claim in more detail, and discuss the implications of it in Saul (2002*a*).

abilities, since my letter looks perfectly cooperative to them—I have given them precisely the information that they asked for. Grice's second necessary condition for conversational implicature, then, fails to be met. So I have not implicated that Darren doesn't have much to recommend him as a philosopher.

Another way of seeing that I did not implicate this is to consider Grice's calculability requirement. My intended implicature was not calculable, simply because it was not possible for my audience to work it out from what I said, drawing only on the conversational maxims and their background knowledge. I clearly did not conversationally implicate it, then.

My intended implicature was also neither said nor conventionally implicated—it strays too far from the linguistic meanings of any of the sentences in my letter. Yet nonetheless, I did surely mean it. This claim, then—that Darren doesn't have much to recommend him as a philosopher—is something that I meant but neither said nor implicated. The fact that it is a part of what I mean despite fitting neither of these categories suffices to show that (SME) is false. However, the example in 4.3.2.2 will show us that there are other ways for (SME) to fail.

4.3.2.2.1 A misguided objection
One might worry that there is something illegitimate about using a case like this as an objection to (SME).

Speaker Meaning Exhaustiveness (SME): Speaker meaning divides exhaustively into what is said and what is implicated.

The worry derives from the fact that the speaker in the example above is clearly not relevantly well-informed. There is crucial information—about the nature of the job Darren is applying for—that I lack. As I have noted, (SMT) must be restricted to the intuitions of the competent, rational, and relevantly well-informed.

Speaker Meaning Tracking (SMT): The truth-conditional intuitions of competent, rational speakers who are fully informed of relevant facts track speaker meaning.

Surely, one might think, similar considerations should apply to (SME). If this is right, then (SME) should be a principle that only applies to what is meant by competent, rational, and relevantly well-informed speakers. This would surely rule out the case above, thus leaving an appropriately restricted (SME) standing.

This worry, however, is misguided. The first reason for supposing it to be misguided may at first seem not very interesting. This reason derives differences in how I have generated (SMT) and (SME). (SMT) is not a principle that I have drawn from the literature. Instead, it is a part of my attempt to provide a plausible motivation for assuming (SOI). (SME), on the other hand, is different. It is both explicitly stated and widely endorsed in the literature, as we have already noted. It is never restricted to just the competent, rational, and relevantly well-informed. The example above is, then, a counter-example to (SME), even though it involves a speaker who lacks relevant information.

The above response may well seem uncompelling. Surely, one might think, I am being extremely uncharitable to those who have endorsed (SME). Even if they failed to state that (SME) applies only to the competent, rational, and relevantly well-informed it could well be—it might seem—that proponents really did intend such a restriction.

I think this move, appealing though it may at first seem, is not a good one. Again, a contrast between (SMT) and (SME) is helpful. (SMT) concerns the intuitions that guide us in our theorising about language. It is very natural to suppose that we do not want our theorising to be guided by the intuitions of the incompetent, the irrational, and the misinformed. When we encounter such intuitions, we can (and should) explain them away as arising from incompetence, irrationality, and misinformation. Given that we can explain the intuitions in this way, we need not and should not let them guide our theorising. Thus, the restrictions built into (SMT) are reasonable ones. (SME) is quite a different matter. It is a claim not about intuitions but about the nature of speaker meaning. Some speakers simply *are* incompetent, irrational, or misinformed. One who hopes to understand speaker meaning needs to understand what these speakers mean, and not only what more fortunate speakers mean. It seems especially difficult to treat misinformed speakers as an aberration. Misinformation and the miscommunication that can sometimes result are far too widespread for theorists to ignore. Restricting (SME) in a manner parallel to (SMT) would, then, be a serious mistake.

4.3.2.3 *Attempted saying*

The next example is one in which the speaker (it seems) attempts to say something, but fails to do so. What he means by his utterance is, as a result, neither said nor implicated. Again, we see that (SME) is false.

On 27 November 2002, George W. Bush uttered the following sentence:[12]

(1) The law I sign today directs new funds and new focus to the task of collecting vital intelligence on terrorist threats and on weapons of mass *production*. [Emphasis mine]

Presumably, what Bush meant was (1*).

(1*) The law I sign today directs new funds and new focus to the task of collecting vital intelligence on terrorist threats and on weapons of mass *destruction*. [Emphasis mine]

According to Grice, however, as to most theorists, Bush did not *say* what (1*) conventionally means, because he uttered the wrong sentence. Nor did he implicate it—he certainly did not think that the audience could work out from his utterance of (1) that he meant something better captured by (1*), and this means that Grice's third necessary condition for implicating was not met.[13] And it is clear that (1) does not carry (1*) as a conventional implicature. It is wrong, then, to suppose that speaker meaning divides exhaustively into what is said and what is implicated.

So where does this leave the argument I constructed on behalf of (SOI)?

- (SMT): The truth-conditional intuitions of competent, rational speakers who are fully informed of relevant facts track speaker meaning.
- (SME): Speaker meaning divides exhaustively into what is said and what is implicated.
- So (one might think), (SOI): For an utterance of a sentence S in a context C, the truth-conditional intuitions of competent, rational speakers who are relevantly well-informed must match the truth conditions of either what is said or what is implicated by S in C.

(SME) is false. (SOI) begins to indeed look substantially less well-supported once we abandon (SME): it is simply much less plausible to assume that any errors in our (rational, competent, fully informed)

---

[12] Jacob Weisberg, *Slat*. Available at: http://slate.msn.com/id/76886/

[13] The calculability condition may, however, be met: arguably, it *is* calculable that Bush must have meant what's expressed by (1*). The audience can work out, from Bush's utterance and the relevant background beliefs, that this must have been what he was trying to say, and therefore that this was what he meant.

intuitions must be due to what is implicated. Even if we assume that our intuitions must track some element of speaker meaning, the considerations above show that there is much more to speaker meaning than just what is said and what is implicated. So even if (SMT) is true, the failure of (SME) should convince us not to accept (SOI).

4.3.3 Saving (SME)

There may, however, be a way to save the claim that speaker meaning divides exhaustively into what is said and what is implicated (SME). We can do this by abandoning some of what Grice says about saying and implicating. We can maintain the exhaustiveness claim by taking *it* as fundamental to understanding implicature—that is, by insisting that what is implicated really is just whatever the speaker means but does not say. Speaker meaning really does divide exhaustively into what is said and what is implicated, on this view, because anything that is meant by the speaker but not said is implicated. Our original considerations in favour of (SOI) will thus be resurrected: if we combine this understanding of implicature with the idea that our intuitions track speaker meaning, it will be natural to suppose that our intuitions must match either what is said or what is implicated.

The counterexamples to (SME) no longer apply. When I wrote my letter of reference, I meant but did not say that that Darren doesn't have much to recommend him as a philosopher. On the current view, this suffices for implicating that Darren doesn't have much to recommend him as a philosopher. When Bush uttered a sentence including the phrase 'weapons of mass production', he meant but did not say something about weapons of mass destruction. This suffices for him to implicate something about weapons of mass destruction.

This understanding of 'implicature', as a catch-all term for what is meant but not said, seems in some ways a plausible one to attribute to many of those who write on implicature. After all, they say that speaker meaning dividing exhaustively into what is said and what is implicated, and often offer helpful tree diagrams showing this (Levinson 1983: 131; Horn 1992: 165; Neale 1992.) But it is important to note that it is in other ways a very implausible understanding to attribute to these writers. The reason is that along with the exhaustiveness claim, they also present, for example, Grice's necessary conditions for conversational implicature. These conditions, as we have seen, have the effect of blocking certain claims that are meant but not said from counting as implicatures. (This shows the claims are not conversational implicatures; it is obvious that they are not conventional implicatures.) Moreover, although many writers do not place much emphasis on Grice's necessary conditions for conversational implicature (despite presenting them), they do generally place a great deal of emphasis on his calculability criterion—and we have already seen (in the Darren case) that the calculability criterion, on its own, is sufficient to block the possibility of speaker meaning dividing exhaustively into what is said and what is implicated. To maintain this new understanding of implicature, then, the calculability requirement for conversational implicature must be dropped.

It is important to appreciate the consequences of this new version of implicature. On this new version, traditional tests like calculability are utterly irrelevant to discerning the presence of an implicature. All that matters is, when it comes to implicating that P, is that the speaker means that P without saying it. This means that it is much, much easier to defend an implicature-based explanation of intuitions. A defender of Naïve Implicature theory, for example, need devote no time at all to demonstrating calculability, and a detractor cannot object that the suggested implicature fails to be calculable. This nullifies—for example—Recanati's and Schiffer's objections (mentioned in Chapter 1), which derive from Grice's calculability requirement.

The suggested understanding, then, is quite a revisionary one. Nonetheless, it is a perspective from which (SOI) may indeed seem a sensible limitation.

(SOI): For an utterance of a sentence S in a context C, the truth-conditional intuitions of competent, rational speakers who are relevantly well-informed must match the truth conditions of either what is said or what is implicated by S in C.

Any mistake in our truth-conditional intuitions, on this view, must be due to what is implicated—as either what is said or what is implicated must have truth conditions that match those indicated by our intuitions. After all, our intuitions are about what the speaker means, and anything the speaker means but does not say must be implicated.

4.3.3.1 Do we now have support for (SOI)?

I have noted that (SMT) and (SME) seem, together, to provide good reason to believe (SOI).

- (SMT): The truth-conditional intuitions of competent, rational speakers who are fully informed of relevant facts track speaker meaning.
- (SME): Speaker meaning divides exhaustively into what is said and what is implicated.
- (SOI): For an utterance of a sentence S in a context C, the truth-conditional intuitions of competent, rational speakers who are relevantly well-informed must match the truth conditions of either what is said or what is implicated by S in C.

I think it is very natural, if one accepts (SMT) and (SME), to suppose that (SOI) must be true. Thus, one who is willing to accept the understanding of implicature suggested above (on which (SME) is true) may well seem to have reason to accept (SOI). However, I think that making the move from (SMT) and (SME) to (SOI) is a serious mistake.

Before I look at why this move is a mistake, it is worth recalling that we should not be surprised to find that (SMT) and (SME) fail to support (SOI), even on the understanding of implicature suggested above. The reason for this is simple: we have already seen that (SOI) is false on this understanding of implicature. If (SMT) and (SME) seem appealing, then, we should want to make sense of the idea that they fail to support (SOI). In Chapter 3, we considered the idea that anything meant but not said is implicated. There we saw that this understanding of implicature still fails to help us in accommodating simple sentence intuitions. On this understanding, a speaker cannot implicate that p unless they mean that p. But we saw that intuitions are not sensitive to the speaker's meaning in the way that they would need to be, if they were to be explained as due to implicature, understood in this way. More specifically, we saw that that our intuitions about Lois's utterance of (2) do not change when we learn that Lois was unenlightened, and therefore unable to mean any proposition involving aspects.

(2) Superman leaps more tall buildings than Clark Kent does.

Our intuitions about (2), then, cannot be explained as due to our grasping some implicated intuition-matching proposition. Since we know (SOI) to be false on the understanding of implicature suggested above, then, we should not be surprised at all to find that this definition of implicature, accompanied by (SMT) and (SME), fails to provide good support for (SOI).

But why do we lack support for (SOI), when (SMT) and (SME) appear to provide reasons for believing (SOI)? Let's look a little more closely at why one might suppose that (SMT) and (SME) support (SOI).

- (SMT): The truth-conditional intuitions of speakers who are competent, rational, and relevantly well-informed track speaker meaning.
- (SME): Speaker meaning divides exhaustively into what is said and what is implicated.
- So, (SOI): For an utterance of a sentence S in a context C, the truth-conditional intuitions of competent, rational speakers who are relevantly well-informed must match the truth conditions of either what is said or what is implicated by S in C.

This argument is not, as we have already noted, valid. And yet, it does seem to have intuitive pull. It seems to me that the intuitive pull comes from a train of thought something like the following. Our intuitions track speaker meaning, which divides exhaustively into two parts, each of which has its own truth conditions. Because these two components may differ from one another, it doesn't make sense to discuss the truth conditions of what the speaker means. They may mean more than one thing—what they say and what they implicate—and these may have different truth conditions. Our truth-conditional intuitions, then, will *really* be either about the truth conditions of what is said or about the truth conditions of what is implicated. Since our truth-conditional intuitions must be about either what is said or what is implicated, they must match either what is said or what is implicated.

But this train of thought is flawed. Even if our intuitions must be *about* either what is said or what is implicated, it seems to me that there is no guarantee that these intuitions will *correctly* reflect the truth conditions of that which they are about. After all, these are *our* intuitions—surely they may be affected by facts about our psychology. The intuitions that I have about what is said or what is implicated may be affected not only by what is said or what is implicated, but also by facts about the way that I process what is said or what is implicated. Grasping what is said or implicated is one thing; correctly evaluating its truth conditions is another. And there is no reason to suppose that one who accomplishes the first will always accomplish the second.[14] All this is so, moreover, even when we consider competent, rational speakers. In

---

[14] It seems to me that one might also worry about what it means for intuitions to 'track speaker meaning'. I am assuming that it means, roughly, that our intuitions are due to what we take the speaker's meaning to be. However, one might wonder about this idea a bit: do we really form convictions about what the speaker means, and base our intuitions on these views? Clearly not. One who wanted to defend (SMT) would need to say a great deal more about what it means to say that our intuitions track speaker meaning. However, I am not in the business of defending (SMT). Instead, I am merely

chapters to come, I will return to this point, describing in more detail the ways that intuitions regarding some proposition's truth conditions may fail to reflect that proposition's truth conditions. At the moment, I merely wish to call attention to this possibility.

Even if we accept an understanding of implicature that supports (SME), then, and we accept (SMT), we do not have good reason to accept (SOI).

4.4 AUDIENCE INTERPRETATION PERSPECTIVE

So far, we have discussed a perspective that focuses on language users as speakers, trying to communicate what they mean. An alternative perspective focuses on language users as audiences, interpreting utterances. A theorist who takes this as their focus will concern themself with the psychological processes audiences use in utterance interpretation. From this perspective, then, our truth-conditional intuitions are tracking not the speaker's meaning but the audience's interpretation of the utterance. Relevance Theorists (e.g. Wilson and Sperber 1981) offer an interpretation of Grice that takes him to share this focus. According to their increasingly popular interpretation of Grice, *audience interpretation* divides exhaustively into what is said and what is implicated. Wilson and Sperber claim that Grice means the distinction between what is said and what is implicated to be crucial to understanding audience interpretation, and that Grice takes it that 'every aspect of interpretation can be assigned to one or the other category' (1981: 156). For one who endorses the view they attribute to Grice,[15] it may seem plausible to suppose that any mistakes in our intuitions must be due to what is implicated. If our intuitions are about the audience's interpretation, and the audience's interpretation divides exhaustively into what is said and what is implicated, then (it may seem) our intuitions should match up with either what is said or what is implicated.

Putting these ideas in a way that parallels our discussion of the speaker meaning perspective, we arrive at:

using it in an attempt to understand how it is that one might be drawn to a principle like (SOI).

[15] It is worth emphasising that Relevance Theorists themselves definitely do not endorse the view they attribute to Grice. Indeed, I'm not sure anyone does.

- Audience Interpretation Tracking (AIT): The truth-conditional intuitions of competent, rational speakers who are fully informed of relevant facts track the audience's interpretation.[16]
- Audience Interpretation Exhaustiveness (AIE): The audience's interpretation divides exhaustively into what is said and what is implicated.

The current suggestion is that (AIT) and (AIE) provide support for (SOI):

(SOI) For an utterance of a sentence S in a context C, the truth-conditional intuitions of competent, rational speakers who are relevantly well-informed must match the truth conditions of either what is said or what is implicated by S in C.

In the next sections, I show that (AIE) is false. I show this by offering two examples in which (AIE) fails. After this, I offer a revisionary understanding of implicature that would allow one to maintain (AIE). But I follow this by showing that even if one accepts (AIT) and (AIE), one does not have good reason to accept (SOI). Some of my arguments will parallel those made in my discussion of the Speaker Meaning Perspective. Accordingly, I will deal with them a bit more quickly.

4.4.1 Problems

4.4.1.1 Audience wrong about what is implicated

Our first case is one in which the audience takes the speaker to implicate something that the speaker does not, according to Grice's understanding, implicate. This, then, is a case in which there is a part of the audience's interpretation that falls neither into the *said* category nor the *implicated* category. That is, this case shows (AIE) to fail.

Audience Interpretation Exhaustiveness (AIE): The audience's interpretation divides exhaustively into what is said and what is implicated.

I am writing a letter of reference for Ethelred, whom I believe to be a very talented philosopher. However, I know that Ethelred has had a lot of trouble on the philosophy job market, and I believe him to be applying for a job as a waiter. So I write a letter describing only how prompt, reliable, friendly, and well-groomed Ethelred is, taking

---

[16] The need for 'competent', 'rational' and 'fully informed' perfectly parallels the considerations that moved us to adopt (SMT) in the discussion of the Speaker Meaning Perspective.

this to be the information needed by those reviewing his application. Unfortunately, however, it turns out that Ethelred is applying for a job in philosophy. The committee reading my letter decides that the letter makes no sense unless they assume me to think Ethelred is a terrible philosopher, so they take me to be conversationally implicating this. They are, however, wrong. I did not think that the audience would or even could work out from my letter that I thought Ethelred was a terrible philosopher. (If I had, I would not have written the letter that I wrote.) Grice's third necessary condition, then, is not met: I did not conversationally implicate that Ethelred was a terrible philosopher. Yet this claim is nonetheless part of the audience's interpretation. Since it is clearly neither said nor conventionally implicated, we can conclude that the audience's interpretation includes a claim that is neither said nor implicated: (AIE) fails.

4.4.1.2 Audience wrong about what is said [17]

Audiences may also be wrong about what is said, and this too may lead to failures of (AIE).

Audience Interpretation Exhaustiveness (AIE): The audience's interpretation divides exhaustively into what is said and what is implicated.

As an illustration, consider the following notable case, which occurred in London in 1999. A black actress and singer, Patti Boulaye, who was running for office as a Conservative Party candidate, was quoted as having uttered sentence (3).[18]

(3) This is the time to support apartheid because it is unfashionable.

The sentence she actually uttered was (3*).

---

[17] This example is taken, with minor alterations, from Saul (2002*b*), and used with kind permission of Springer Science and Business Media.

[18] The correction, from the *Guardian*, 18 March 1999, reads as follows:

. . . In the course of the article we quoted Ms Boulaye . . . as saying: 'This is a time to support apartheid . . . I mean people say "Why didn't you support it when it was in government?" Because it would have been the fashionable thing to do so. This is the time to support apartheid because its unfashionable'. What Ms Boulaye actually said was 'a party', meaning the Conservative Party. At no time during the interview was apartheid mentioned. The journalist concerned misheard Ms Boulaye's remarks but then asked no follow up questions about what she thought she heard. The offense was compounded by the picking out of part of these misheard remarks as a subsidiary heading . . .

Boulaye later successfully sued for libel.

(3*) This is the time to support a party because it is unfashionable.

The audience, a *Guardian* reporter, took Boulaye to have said what is generally said by utterances of (3).[19] But, according to both common sense and Grice's theory, this is not what she said. For Grice, this fails to be said both because Boulaye did not intend it and because it is not what the sentence that she uttered means. We have, then, a case in which the audience is wrong about what is said. It is perhaps worth noting further that an audience may be wrong about both what is said and what is implicated, at the same time. Indeed, this is likely to happen when an audience is wrong about what is said. In the example above, the reporter might well have taken Boulaye to be implicating that she supports apartheid. Since, however, Boulaye did not think that the audience could work this out from her utterance (to put it mildly), Grice's third necessary condition for conversational implicature failed to be fulfilled. Boulaye did not implicate that she supported apartheid, and the audience was therefore wrong about what was implicated.[20]

On Grice's theory, then, audiences may sometimes be wrong both about what is said and about what is implicated. This is really not very surprising, and it in fact accords perfectly with common sense. But this not very surprising fact has the important consequence that we can rule out any claim that audience interpretation divides exhaustively into what is said and what is implicated. (AIE), then is false. Since (AIE) is false, we no longer seem to have good reason to accept (SOI).

(SOI) For an utterance of a sentence S in a context C, the truth-conditional intuitions of competent, rational speakers who are relevantly well-informed must match the truth conditions of either what is said or what is implicated by S in C.

If audience interpretation does not divide exhaustively into what is said and what is implicated, then it is clear that intuitions that track audience interpretation need not concern either what is said or what

---

[19] I'm abstracting here from issues regarding indexical reference, as they are not relevant to the point.

[20] One might well suppose that cases of mis-hearing should be treated as special, and perhaps not included in the claim that every part of the audience's interpretation must be said or implicated. If this is done, then the Boulaye example no longer counts against (AIE). However, the Ethelred example in 4.4.1.1 still serves to defeat it.

is implicated—as there is much more to audience interpretation than
these two elements.

4.4.2 An alternative understanding of implicature: audience interpretation minus what is said

A proponent of the audience interpretation perspective can still salvage
(AIE).

Audience Interpretation Exhaustiveness (AIE): The audience's interpretation
divides exhaustively into what is said and what is implicated.

She can do this by adopting an understanding of 'implicature' on which
any part of the audience's interpretation that is not said is implicated.
On this understanding, (AIE) will clearly be true. This understanding
of 'implicature' is what Relevance Theorists sometimes seem to be
suggesting.[21] Although I do not take this to be Relevance Theorists'
considered view, and I do not know of anyone else who clearly holds this
view, it is worth at least brief consideration.[22] On this understanding,
then, any proposition that is neither said nor conventionally implicated
will presumably be conversationally implicated. If this understanding
of implicature is adopted, then my examples above cannot show that
the audience's interpretation fails to divide into what is said and what is
implicated.[23]

---

[21] If we read 'explicate' as 'say', which is required to make sense of many of their
claims comparing relevance theoretic accounts to Gricean ones. One example of this
is Carston's (1991: 45) claim that 'those who wish to maintain an implicature analysis
have to say that the alleged temporal . . . implicatures [involving "and"] contribute to
the truth conditions of the utterance in which they occur, that is, to the explicit content
(what is said) since they follow Grice in the view that the explicature is another term for
the truth-conditional content of the utterance'.

[22] Sometimes Relevance Theorists seem to hold a different view, on which what is
said and what is implicated must also be intended by the speaker. On this view, neither
audience interpretation nor speaker meaning will divide exhaustively into what is said
and what is implicated. See Saul (2002*b*) for more discussion of this view.

[23] It is worth noting that Relevance Theorists also have a rather expansive conception
of saying ('explicating', in their terminology). For them, what is said may go well beyond
the linguistic meaning of the sentence uttered. So, for example, one who utters 'he
went to the edge of the cliff and jumped' may well say roughly what is said by 'he
went to the edge of the cliff and jumped *off the edge of the cliff*'. This fact about their
view, however, is not relevant to the present discussion: nobody would maintain that
the problematic claims in the examples discussed in this section are said, even on this
expansive understanding of saying. For more on Relevance Theorists' conception of what
is said, see Saul (2002*b*).

Consider first the example in which I falsely believed Ethelred to be applying for a job as a waiter, and I wrote only about attributes relevant to being a waiter. The audience took me to have conversationally implicated that Ethelred was a poor philosopher. Because Grice's third necessary condition failed to be met, I claimed that I did not in fact conversationally implicate this. However, now we have abandoned Grice's conditions for conversational implicature, and instead adopted a new understanding. Since I clearly neither said nor conventionally implicated that Ethelred is a poor philosopher, I conversationally implicated it—despite the fact that I never would have imagined the audience would take me to have done so. This result is a bit counterintuitive, and certainly at odds with most thinking on conversational implicature.

Now consider the example of Patti Boulaye's misreported utterance. Boulaye clearly did not say that it was the time to support apartheid; nor did she conventionally implicate it. However, this claim was a part of the audience's interpretation of her utterance. On the current view, then, it was conversationally implicated—despite the fact that Boulaye certainly didn't think that the audience would work it out from her utterance. But it seems very strange to say that Boulaye implicated this. At the very least, this case shows just how revisionary the proposed understanding of conversational implicature would be.

If one is willing to accept these difficulties, (AIE) can be maintained, allowing the argument from (AIT) and (AIE) to (SOI) to be resurrected:

- (AIT): The truth-conditional intuitions of competent, rational speakers who are fully informed of relevant facts track the audience's interpretation.
- (AIE): The audience's interpretation divides exhaustively into what is said and what is implicated.
- So, (SOI): For an utterance of a sentence S in a context C, the truth-conditional intuitions of competent, rational speakers who are relevantly well-informed must match the truth conditions of either what is said or what is implicated by S in C.

The idea behind this argument is, structurally, a familiar one: If our intuitions concern the audience's interpretation, and the audience's interpretation divides exhaustively into what is said and what is implicated, it will be natural to suppose that our intuitions must be tracking either what is said or what is implicated. Any mistakes must be due to mistaking what is implicated for what is said. So our intuitions must match either what is said or what is implicated.

As with the parallel argument from the Speaker Meaning Perspective, however, we should not expect this argument to succeed: Simple sentences show the conclusion of this argument to be false, even under the current revisionary understanding of 'implicature'. A brief reminder: in Chapter 3, we examined the suggestion that any aspect of the audience's interpretation that is not said must be implicated. There we saw that this understanding of implicature cannot help us to save (SOI). We saw that we have truth-conditional intuitions that really do not seem to reflect the audience's state of mind in the way required to uphold (SOI). The example that showed this involved Lois uttering (4) to Miles.

(4) Superman leaps more tall buildings than Clark Kent does.

Intuitively, (4) is true, and this intuition does not disappear if we are told that Miles is unenlightened. But, we saw, there is no intuition-matching proposition that could form a part of an unenlightened person's interpretation of Lois's utterance. So there can be no proposition, said or implicated, that matches our intuitions—even on the current revisionary understanding of 'implicature'. (SOI), then, must be false.

The initially appealing audience-oriented argument for (SOI) goes wrong in exactly the same way that the speaker-oriented one did. *Even if* our truth-conditional intuitions are about either what is said or what is implicated, we cannot assume that our intuitions must match either what is said or what is implicated. Our intuitions are *ours*, and facts about our psychology play a role in producing them. There is no reason to assume that they must be a correct reflection of either what is said or what is implicated—even if we are competent, rational, and fully informed. This sort of worry will turn out to be very important when we come to developing a positive view.

4.5 STRANGENESS OF (EOI)

Expressed or Implicated (EOI): For an utterance of a sentence S in a context C, the truth-conditional intuitions of competent, rational speakers who are relevantly well-informed must match the truth conditions of either what is (semantically) expressed or what is implicated by S in C.

However plausible and appealing (EOI) may initially look, we should not be surprised to find that the motivations we have examined for adopting it fall short of success. It is actually rather a strange assumption to make, as we have begun to see. I think the idea that (EOI) is odd also gains plausibility from a bit of reflection on some psychological data. Although psychologists do sometimes postulate implicatures as a source of error regarding truth conditions, they also look to *many other possible sources of error* (even for rational, well-informed subjects). We will examine just two examples here: the Wason selection task and the Moses illusion.

4.5.1 Wason[24]

The Wason selection task involves—in its broadest outline—asking people to judge which facts they need to know in order to evaluate the truth of a conditional statement. Wason's original task (Wason 1966) presented subjects with cards that they were told had a letter on one side and a number on the other. The cards were presented in such a way that subjects could see only one side. They were then asked to say which cards they would need to turn over in order to determine whether the experimenter was speaking truthfully when she said, 'if a card has a vowel on one side, then it has an even number on the other side' (Wason 1966: 146). People are, in general, very bad at this task. They make terrible decisions as to which information they would need to decide whether the claim in question is true or false.[25] There is an enormous literature on this task, and there are many, many explanations of why people make the mistakes that they do. Some do turn on pragmatics, but others involve cheater-detection modules, availability effects, confirmation biases, matching biases, and reasoning schemas—to name just a few.[26] The judgments called for in the Wason test are judgments about what information is relevant to a decision regarding truth-value. Nonetheless, implicature-based explanations are just one sort among many that have been offered for the Wason reasoning error. If errors in deciding *what is relevant* to decisions about truth value can be explained in such a broad variety of ways, it seems plausible to suppose that there may be a similar variety of explanations

---

[24] The material in this section is taken, with minor alterations, from Braun and Saul (2002), with kind permission of Springer Science and Business Media.

[25] There are, however, certain logically equivalent tasks on which people perform very well.

[26] For a good overview of approaches to the Wason selection task, see Evans et al. (1993).

available for errors in decisions about truth values themselves. The wide range of possible errors considered by psychologists suggests that philosophers attempting to explain truth-conditional intuitions may unduly limit themselves by focussing only on what is expressed and what is implicated.[27]

4.5.2 The Moses illusion[28]

The Moses illusion is best presented by example.[29] Try to answer this question:

(26) How many animals of each kind did Moses take on the ark?

If you are like most readers, you answered 'two'. But, of course, that answer is incorrect, for it was Noah, not Moses, who took animals into the ark (according to the Biblical story). What makes your answer puzzling is that you *knew* this fact about Noah (and Moses). Most people similarly tend to judge that sentence (27) is true, even though they 'know better'.

(27) Moses took two animals of each kind on the ark

On the other hand, people tend not to make these mistakes when the name 'Nixon' is substituted for 'Moses' in either sentence. Experiments strongly suggest that readers correctly understand the relevant sentences (including the name) and that they are not misled by conversational implicatures. If this is so, then there is some error taking place that has nothing to do with implicatures; and Moses cases constitute clear counterexamples to (EOI). Nearly all psychologists who have studied this phenomenon agree that the correct explanation involves the fact that most people associate similar features with the names 'Moses' and 'Noah', for instance, being a Biblical character, receiving messages from God, and performing important deeds involving water (Moses

[27] Consideration of cases like this may also lead one to doubt the appropriateness of assuming that intuitions are to be explained in terms of *any* intuition-matching proposition. I think such doubts are wholly appropriate, but in this chapter my goal is the fairly modest one of arguing that it is wrong to assume that intuitions must be explained in terms of expressed or implicated intuition-matching propositions.

[28] The material in this section is taken, with minor alterations, from Braun and Saul (2002), with kind permission from Springer Science and Business Media.

[29] The Moses illusion was first studied (and named) in Erickson and Mattson (1981). Subsequent studies include Reder and Kusbit (1991); Kamas et al. (1996); and Hannon and Daneman (2001).

parted the Red Sea). According to one explanation (Reder and Kusbit 1991), the overlap of features associated with the two names causes readers to make errors when they draw on their memories to answer the (correctly understood) question or to evaluate the truth of the (correctly understood) indicative sentence.

In these experiments, subjects' mistakes are clearly not due to factual ignorance. So, as with our own intuitions about simple sentences, another explanation must be sought. But, as we have seen, explanations involving implicatures are only one sort among many that psychologists consider. This suggests, it seems to me, that we philosophers may have a tendency to unduly limit ourselves. Truth-conditional intuitions are determined by complex psychological processes. Prima facie, any number of factors could throw these intuitions off. For instance, when you decide whether some utterance of (2) is true or false, given a certain set of facts, you are influenced by (at least) which facts you take to be relevant and what you take their relevance to be; how well you recall relevant background facts; how long and hard you think about background facts; and any number of biases and the like. Or you may be influenced by connections between features you associate with a name in a sentence and those you associate with some other sentence (as subjects in the Moses experiment seem to be). There is no reason to assume that errors in truth-conditional intuitions could only be due to a confusion of what is expressed with what is implicated. (EOI) does not, then, seem likely to be true.[30] In Chapter 6, we will look in more detail at psychological results indicating factors that might influence intuitions about simple sentences.

4.6 CONCLUSION

In the previous chapters, we surveyed accounts that attempt to explain our truth-conditional intuitions about utterances of simple sentences as resulting from some proposition, expressed or implicated, whose truth conditions match those that we intuitively assign to the utterances. All of these accounts failed. So in this chapter, we examined the motivation

---

[30] Again, consideration of this example may lead one to doubt more than just the truth of (EOI). It may—and probably should—lead one to doubt that intuitions must be explained in terms of intuition-matching propositions, even if these propositions are not required to be expressed or implicated. I agree with this thought, and will discuss it at some length in the chapters to come.

for restricting our theoretical options to just accounts of these sorts. That is, we examined the principle (EOI) and how its acceptance might be motivated. In particular, we looked at arguments that might make (EOI), or its more Gricean correlate (SOI), appear to be plausible. We saw that key premises of these arguments were false. We then considered new understandings of implicature on which these premises would be true. It turned out not only that these new understandings brought with them new and serious difficulties, but also that the arguments for (SOI) were not, on closer inspection, nearly so appealing as they first appeared. They should really never have been taken to provide support for (SOI). We saw that psychologists do not seem to assume the truth of any principle like this, a fact that called attention to the many and various complex psychological processes that may play a role in producing our intuitions. As far as I can tell, there is no reason at all to suppose that the truth conditions indicated by our intuitions must match those of either what is expressed or what is implicated. In the next chapters we will consider the prospects for accommodating simple sentence intuitions once we abandon the limitation to what is expressed and what is implicated.

5

Abandoning (EOI)

In this chapter, I begin to look for solutions to the Enlightenment Problem. The natural place to start such a search is with accounts that reject the problematic assumption discussed in the last chapter, (EOI).

Expressed or Implicated (EOI): For an utterance of a sentence S in a context C, the truth-conditional intuitions of competent, rational speakers who are relevantly well-informed must match the truth conditions[1] of either what is (semantically) expressed or what is implicated by S in C.

Although there has been a widespread tendency to offer theories that accord with (EOI), this has by no means been universal. There are theories that conflict with (EOI), and here we will look at some of these. What we will see, however, is that some ways of deviating from (EOI) really do not deviate very far. Some such theories remain extremely close to (EOI) in spirit. In this chapter I examine two otherwise very different ways of accommodating intuitions, those offered by Scott Soames (2002) and Kent Bach (1994). Although neither of these theorists has written on simple sentences, their general semantic and pragmatic frameworks make available new forms of responses to simple sentences, ones that would involve violating (EOI).[2] It turns out, however, that these responses too fall victim to the Enlightenment Problem. This helps us to begin to see more clearly what it is that gives rise to the Enlightenment Problem. At the end of this chapter, I begin looking for accounts that move yet further away from the picture that gives rise to this problem. In this chapter, I will consider and reject one such account. In the next chapter, I move toward more viable solutions to the problems posed by simple sentences.[3]

---

[1] Recall that by 'truth conditions' I mean actual truth value and truth values when evaluated in other possible worlds.

[2] Although these responses are *available* to these theorists, I am not claiming that they would endorse such accounts.

[3] Thomas Ede Zimmerman (2005) has proposed an account that may also violate (EOI), although this is not entirely clear. According to him, anti-substitution intuitions

5.1 BACH: ELEMENTS OF SPEAKER MEANING

Kent Bach rejects the idea that one's options in semantic and pragmatic theorising should be restricted to what is semantically expressed and what is implicated. Bach, then, rejects (EOI). For Bach, 'what is said' refers to what is semantically expressed. Because the proper understanding of 'what is said' is a matter of intense controversy, and because Bach and Soames use the phrase very differently, I am going to avoid it in my discussions of both accounts. For clarity's sake, I have replaced Bach's uses of 'what is said' with 'what is expressed'.

> The situation may be described in Gricean terms: the distinction between what is [expressed] and what is implicated is not exhaustive. (Bach 1994: 124)

For Bach, what is expressed is to be identified with semantic content. And semantic content is tightly constrained by linguistic meaning. As Bach explains it:

> . . . if any element of the content of an utterance, i.e., of what the speaker intends to convey, does not correspond to any element of the sentence being uttered, it is not part of what is [expressed]. (Bach 2001*a*: 15)

Bach holds that what speakers mean—what they intend to convey—is often *not* what their utterances semantically express.[4] What speakers mean, for Bach, generally includes far more than what is semantically expressed. Conversational implicatures are one sort of thing that speakers mean beyond what is semantically expressed. Another, however, are conversational implic*i*tures (Bach's own term).

---

about names that *have changed* (like 'Leningrad'/'St Petersburg') are to be dealt with semantically while others should be dealt with pragmatically. On his pragmatic story, an enlightened audience would understand a speaker known to be enlightened who utters 'Superman leaps more tall buildings than Clark Kent' as conveying roughly *I would have said 'Superman leaps more tall buildings than Clark Kent' if I had believed that the bearers of 'Superman' and 'Clark Kent' were distinct*. But this runs into problems. Imagine an enlightened speaker who has been wrongly informed that Lois found the reporter look far more attractive than the Superhero look, and that this affected her sex life. This speaker says 'Lois slept with Clark but she didn't sleep with Superman'. An enlightened audience who knows more about Lois's love life will take this to be false. But Zimmerman's account cannot explain this intuition. According to that account, the speaker conveys *I would have said 'Lois slept with Clark but she didn't sleep with Superman' if I had believed that the bearers of 'Superman' and 'Clark Kent' were distinct*. This proposition is clearly true, so it cannot explain the intuition of falsehood.

   [4] In this, he departs from Grice in an important way. As we noted in Chapter 4, Grice insists that being meant is a necessary condition for being said.

Consider, for example, an utterance of (1).

(1) Jack and Jill are married.

For Bach, (1) semantically expresses a claim that would be true even if Jack and Jill were married to, say, Kevin and Kathy, rather than to each other. But, Bach maintains, a speaker is very unlikely to mean something like that by their utterance of (1). Instead, they will mean something like what is expressed by (1*).

(1*) Jack and Jill are married to each other.

What is expressed by (1*) is what an utterance of (1) would typically carry as a conversational implic*i*ture. It is, roughly, the most minimal proposition that a typical utterer of (1) could be said to mean.

Here is what Bach says about conversational implicitures:

> Implicitures go beyond what is [expressed], but unlike implicatures, which are additional propositions external to what is [expressed], implicitures are built out of what is [expressed]. Even when there is no figurative use of words or phrases, as in metaphor, in impliciture . . . what the sentences mean does not fully determine, even after ambiguities are resolved and indexical references are fixed, what the speaker means. (Bach 1994: 141)

For Bach, then, what speakers mean by their assertive utterances is made up of three elements: (sometimes) what is semantically expressed,[5] conversational implicatures, and conversational implic*i*tures.[6] Implicitures are closely connected to what is expressed, but they go beyond it in the ways that are needed to arrive at a proposition that the speaker means. Implicatures are also meant by the speaker, but they depart yet further from semantic content.

Conversational implicitures, Bach claims, may have a particularly confusing effect on attempts to base semantic theories on intuitions. He writes,

> People's spontaneous judgments or 'intuitions' provide data for semantics, but it is an open question to what extent they reveal semantic facts and should therefore be explained rather than explained away. Since, as I am suggesting, they are often responsive to non-semantic information, to what is implicit in what is [expressed] but not part of it, they should be treated cautiously. (Bach 2001*b*: 23).

---

[5] Recall that, for Bach, what is semantically expressed may be meant by the speaker, but also may not be. He does not take being meant to be a necessary condition for being semantically expressed, although he does take it to be a necessary condition for being implicated or implicited.

[6] Bach denies the existence of conventional implicatures. See Bach (1999).

Intuitions about assertive utterances may reflect not what is expressed but instead conversational implicitures.

To see how this works, consider again a typical utterance of (1). Many people have the intuition that (1) is false if Jack and Jill are married to Kevin and Kathy. Bach maintains that this intuition comes from focusing not on what (1) expresses—a claim that would be true under those circumstances, but instead on what an utterance of (1) is likely to carry as a conversational impliciture—what (1*) expresses. The reason that it is so natural to focus on (1*) according to Bach, is that a speaker is far more likely to mean what (1*) expresses than what (1) expresses. Bach holds that we are often unaware of divergences between what is meant and what is expressed. We must, he says, 'invoke the distinction between what is [expressed] and what is meant, and remember that intuitions tend to be insensitive to that distinction' (Bach 2001*b*: 30).

For a proponent of Bach's view, then, we have not yet canvassed all the options for explaining simple sentence intuitions. In particular, we have neglected the very important category of conversational impliciture. This category is especially important for Bach when it comes to explaining how our intuitions may err. It should not, then, be neglected.

Bach's taxonomy makes way for a new proposal on simple sentences. This is that our truth-conditional intuitions are due not to the semantic content of utterances of simple sentences or to what is implicated by them, but instead to the conversational implicitures that they carry. On this proposal, then, (2) expresses a necessary falsehood—but we take it to be possible for an utterance of (2) to be true because we are focusing not on what (2) expresses but instead on conversational implicitures it might carry.

(2) Superman leaps more tall buildings than Clark Kent.

Although (2)'s semantic content must be false, an utterance of it may carry a conversational impliciture that is true.

In order for this proposal to succeed, we need a proposition with the right truth conditions that might be a conversational impliciture of an utterance of (2). That is, we need a conversational impliciture whose truth conditions match those indicated by our truth-conditional intuitions about (2). These intuitions, as we saw in Chapter 2, display considerable contextual variation: sometimes substitution inferences involving simple sentences seem perfectly acceptable to us and sometimes they don't. We judge utterances of (2) to be true, and (2*) to be false.

(2*) Superman leaps more tall buildings than Superman does.

According to these intuitions, substitution of co-referential names in simple sentences fails. But we also accept some substitution inferences, as with typical utterances of sentences (3) and (3*)

(3) Superman is hungry.
(3*) Clark is hungry.

Moreover, our intuitions about a single sentence may shift with context. Imagine first a context in which we (all of us enlightened) are contrasting the traits that we associate with 'Superman' and 'Clark Kent'—one is bold while the other is shy, one flies while the other does not, one is successful with women while the other is not, and so on. In this context, an utterance of (4) will seem false.

(4) Clark leaps tall buildings.

But now consider a very different context, in which we are all very recently enlightened, and working hard to come to terms with the shocking new facts we have learned about the shy reporter's secret life, by listing off all the things that Clark has secretly been doing. In this context, an utterance of (4) will seem true.

What we need, then, is some intuition-matching proposition that is implicited in the contexts where, intuitively, substitution fails. (For the contexts where substitution intuitively succeeds, we have no such need—the truth conditions indicated by our intuitions match those of what is expressed.) It is hard to see what this proposition could be, other than the sort of proposition Moore and Forbes propose—one that involves aspects or modes of personification. We'll take it, then, that something like (2F) would be the impliciture that we need to explain our intuition that (2) is true.

(2F) Superman, so-personified, leaps more tall buildings than Clark Kent, so-personified.

If an utterance of (2) carried (2F) as an impliciture, we could explain our intuition that this utterance was true: it was due to our focusing not on what the utterance expressed, but rather on its conversational impliciture, something like (2F).

But now remember the case of Lois and Miles. Lois utters (2F) to Miles as an explanation of why Superman seems so much more exciting to her than Clark, and, intuitively, her utterance is true. Our intuitions about this case are, as we saw in Chapters 2 and 3, completely unaffected by information about whether Lois and Miles are enlightened. (This is, of course, the Enlightenment Problem.) Can our Bach-based account cope better with this problem case than the other accounts that we have considered?

In order to explain our intuition that (2) is true as arising from a conversational impliciture like (2F), the Bach-based account would need to claim that this impliciture is present even if Lois and Miles are both unenlightened—since the intuition *is* present in such a case. But (2F) cannot be implicited unless Lois *means* (2F) when she utters (2)—and if she is not enlightened, there is no reason whatsoever for her to intend to convey a proposition about modes of personification (or aspects). After all, if she is unenlightened she will take herself to be speaking about different individuals—why would she *want* to communicate something more complicated?[7]

One might suppose that Bach could reply to this by invoking some category other than implicitures to explain cases in which our intuitions err. But it is important to note that any such explanation, for Bach, must be cast in terms of speaker meaning. Bach's focus, in explaining incorrect intuitions, is consistently on speaker meaning. His methodological cautions are always cast in these terms: we must 'invoke the distinction between what is [expressed] and what is meant, and remember that intuitions tend to be insensitive to that distinction', Bach (2002: 30). So any new intuition-explaining category Bach might postulate looks likely to be some element of speaker meaning. And the example above shows that that this will not work. Our anti-substitution intuitions do not track what speakers mean, or even what they are able to mean—there will be cases, then, in which there is no proposition meant by the speaker that matches the truth conditions indicated by our intuitions. The Enlightenment Problem remains.

5.2 SOAMES: SEMANTIC CONTENT, ASSERTION, IMPLICATURE

5.2.1 Soames's framework

Scott Soames's recent work in *Beyond Rigidity* (2002)—which offers a view very different from his earlier work with Nathan Salmon—can be used to motivate an alternative sort of account of simple sentence intuitions, again one that abandons (EOI).

---

[7] As we saw in Chapter 3 (§3.1.2.2), it is implausible to suppose that all of us—or even just the unenlightened—always mean something aspect-sensitive by such utterances.

Expressed or Implicated (EOI): For an utterance of a sentence S in a context C, the truth-conditional intuitions of competent, rational speakers who are relevantly well-informed must match the truth conditions of either what is (semantically) expressed or what is implicated by S in C.

His taxonomy, like Bach's, is one that allows intuitions to be explained by propositions other than those that are semantically expressed and those that are implicated. For Soames, a third and particularly important alternative is that our intuitions may instead be due to what is asserted.

In *Beyond Rigidity*, Soames contrasts semantic content (what is semantically expressed) with what is asserted. For Soames, the semantic content of a sentence S *is*, roughly, what is asserted by all literal, non-ironic, non-metaphorical utterances of S by competent speakers.[8] The idea here is that any sentence can be used to make a wide variety of assertions, but that there will be a common core to all these assertions — the sentence's semantic content (what is expressed). Soames does not offer a definition of 'assertion'. However, he does give us some necessary conditions for asserting. Here is one relevant passage:

> what an assertive utterance of a sentence s counts as asserting depends not only on the semantic content of s, but also on the obvious background assumptions in the conversation and the speaker's intentions about how the speaker's remark is to be interpreted in the light of them . . . [I]n order for p to be asserted by an utterance of a sentence, it is not enough that conversational participants be in possession of information which together with the speaker's utterance, might, after long or careful consideration, support an inference to p. Rather, the speaker must have reason to believe both that p is a potentially direct, immediate, and relevant inference for all conversational participants, and that the conversational participants recognize this belief of the speaker. (Soames 2002: 79)

An assertive utterance of s, then, will only assert that p if the speaker has reason to believe that (a) the audience could immediately infer that p from the utterance and (b) the audience takes them to believe this. Elsewhere, Soames writes that a speaker must *intend* to convey that p in order to assert p:

> [T]he speaker commits himself to p, in the sense of endorsing p as something to be accepted by members of the conversation; of being responsible to defend p; and of being accountable if p is shown to be false. Intending to undertake such a commitment is a necessary condition for intending to convey p, and hence for asserting p, in the senses of these expressions that I have in mind. (2002: 73)

---

[8] Soames's full characterisation includes qualifications and refinements that are not relevant to our discussion here. For details, see Soames (2002: 55–70).

Slightly confusingly, however, Soames also seems to hold out the possibility that one may assert that *p* even when one does not intend to convey *p*:

[T]he information asserted by an utterance is *standardly* a part of the information that the speaker intends to convey by the utterance. (2002: 72; italics mine)

The above quotation does not seem to fit well with the idea that an intention to convey that *p* is a necessary condition for asserting that *p*. The most charitable way to understand Soames, it seems to me, is to take the passages that seem to commit him to this necessary condition as instead meant merely to commit him to this condition holding *in standard cases*. This immediately raises the issue of when the condition fails to hold. Soames gives us some indication of what circumstances he has in mind as exceptions:

[A] speaker who asserts p thereby intends to convey p, in the sense that I am using these terms (except perhaps in unusual situations in which the speaker is seriously mistaken about what he is asserting, and so does not realize that he is asserting p). (2002: 72)

Soames does not explain what sorts of situations count as ones in which the speaker is seriously mistaken about what they are asserting. It seems most natural to assume that these cases will be ones in which a speaker is importantly mistaken about the linguistic meaning of the sentence that they are assertively uttering. I take it that such cases include those in which the speaker is not fully competent with the words they are using, and possibly those in which they unwittingly utter the wrong words through a slip of the tongue. On this understanding of Soames, such a speaker may still count as asserting the proposition that is the semantic content of the sentence that they utter. So, for example, consider a non-native speaker of Spanish who mistakenly utters (5), when they should have uttered (5*).

(5) Estoy embarazado.
(5*) Estoy azorado.

Such a speaker may unfortunately count as having asserted that they are pregnant—when they intended to assert that they were embarrassed.[9] I will assume, in what follows, that Soames means intending to convey

---

[9] Thanks to Joe Saul for his demonstration of this mistake, and for his willingness to allow me to share it with others.

that *p* to be a necessary condition for asserting that *p except* in cases like this one (and perhaps cases of slips of the tongue).[10]

Soames means assertion to be a very expansive notion. For example, he takes it that, in the right circumstances, a terrorist who utters 'I will detonate my bomb if my demands are not met' may count as asserting that they will kill thousands of people if their demands are not met (2002: 79). Any utterance may assert many propositions, and it may even be indeterminate which proposition is asserted. Thus, assertion is very different from semantic content (what is expressed). Soames takes what is said to be what is asserted. To avoid confusion, I will use only the phrase 'what is asserted' for this notion in my discussion of his view.

Soames argues that intuitions commonly taken to reflect semantic content sometimes reflect instead what is asserted. Most speakers, Soames claims, do not distinguish between these notions when they are asked about what a sentence means, or about whether some utterance is true. Instead, Soames suggests, speakers will tend to focus on what is, or might be, *asserted* by a sentence. Thus, we should not expect intuitions about meaning or truth conditions to be a good guide to the theoretical notion of semantic content—they often reflect instead what is asserted. It is clear from this alone that (EOI) fails on Soames's account: intuitions may be explained as reflecting what is asserted, rather than just what is expressed or what is implicated.

5.2.2 Soames and simple sentences

A Soamesian, then, could offer an alternative explanation of simple sentence intuitions—one on which our mistaken truth-conditional intuitions about utterances of simple sentences are due not to what they implicate, but to what they assert. Our task now is to see whether such a story can succeed.

Soames does not discuss apparent substitution failures in simple sentences. However, his view on apparent substitution failures in belief-reporting utterances is one that could perhaps be adapted to cover simple sentences.[11] According to Soames, a name's contribution to semantic

---

[10] More specifically, I assume above that Soames means the intention condition to apply in normal cases, and that the abnormal cases will be ones in which a speaker utters a sentence whose semantic content is other than they take it to be. I do take this to be the most plausible interpretation of his view. However, I consider an alternative interpretation in footnote 13.

[11] This view is not without its own problems, of course. For a discussion of some of them see Braun (2002); Salmon (2003); Braun and Sider (Forthcoming).

content is always just its referent. As a result, substitution of co-referential names always preserves semantic content and therefore truth conditions. However, he maintains that our name-involving utterances often carry with them assertions beyond their semantic content, and that these asserted propositions—which are descriptive—explain our intuitions. So, for example, consider utterances of (6) and (6*).

(6) Lois believes that Superman can fly.
(6*) Lois believes that Clark can fly.

For Soames, (6)'s truth guarantees the truth of (6*). But this, of course, clashes with the standard intuition that (6*) might be false even if (6) is true. Soames would suggest that our intuition that (6*) is false derives from the fact that utterers of (6*)—which is true (assuming that (6) is true)—typically also assert what is expressed by (6**):

(6**) Lois believes that Clark, the bespectacled reporter, can fly.

(6**) is, of course, false, since Lois doesn't have a belief with the content that Clark, the bespectacled reporter, can fly. (Although she has a belief that consists of Clark and the property of flying, she does not have a belief which consists of Clark, the property of being a bespectacled reporter and flying.) Thus, intuitions that seem to count against substitution of co-referential names in belief reports really derive from mistakenly focusing on what is asserted by belief-reporting utterances.

More generally, Soames maintains that our ordinary utterances of sentences with names in them very often involve the assertion of descriptive propositions. So, for example, in a discussion among a group of disgruntled Democrats, Ray's utterance of (7) may well also assert the semantic content of (7A) or (7B):

(7) Bush wants to launch another invasion.
(7A) Bush, the illegitimate leader, wants to launch another invasion.
(7B) The illegitimate leader wants to launch another invasion.

It is perhaps worth noting that Soames also acknowledges the possibility of an indeterminacy in what is asserted—it may well be indeterminate whether Ray asserted (7A) or (7B), or both.

A first thought on adapting this story to cover simple sentence puzzle cases would be the suggestion that perhaps the descriptive assertions carried by sentences involving names could explain our anti-substitution intuitions about simple sentences. Substitution of co-referential names will always preserve truth conditions, as far as semantic content goes.

But utterances of simple sentences, on this Soamesian story, assert many things beyond their semantic content. An utterance of (2), then, may assert (2A) or (2B); while an utterance of (2*) may assert (2*A) or (2*B)—or both.

(2) Superman leaps more tall buildings than Clark Kent.

(2A) Superman, the caped crusader, leaps more tall buildings than Clark Kent, the bespectacled reporter, does.

(2B) The caped crusader leaps more tall buildings than the bespectacled reporter does.

(2*) Superman leaps more tall buildings than Superman does.

(2*A) Superman, the caped crusader, leaps more tall buildings than Superman, the caped crusader, does.

(2*B) The caped crusader leaps more tall buildings than the caped crusader does.

This suggestion, however, is utterly ineffectual for making sense of our anti-substitution intuitions. Intuition has it that an utterance of (2) can be true. But (2A) is clearly false on Soames's view. (On Soames's view, Superman, the caped crusader, simply *is* Clark Kent, the bespectacled reporter—whatever anyone believes about him—so (2A) is false.) We cannot, then, explain the intuition that (2) is true by taking it to reflect the asserted proposition (2A)'s truth value instead. Things are slightly more complicated with respect to (2B)—if the descriptions are uniquely referring, then (2B) must be false; but if the descriptions do not uniquely refer, (2B) simply lacks a truth value. In neither case, however, is the asserted proposition (2B) true. The intuition that (2) is true, then, is not explained by pointing to one (or both) of these asserted propositions.

A story based on Soames's view of assertion could, however, explain the intuition if a proposition like those that Moore and Forbes take to be expressed is asserted. One suggestion would be, then, that an utterance of (2) that seems true does so because it asserts something like (2F):

(2F) Superman, so-presented, leaps more tall buildings than Clark Kent, so-presented.

(2F), recall, is true—because Superman does leap more tall buildings when presenting himself in the 'Superman'-labelled way than he does when presenting himself in the 'Clark'-labelled way.[12] Since (2F), unlike (2A) and (2B), is true, the intuition that an utterance (2) is true *could* derive from the fact that the utterance in question asserts what (2F) expresses.

---

[12] See Chapter 2, part 2, for details.

But (unsurprisingly, by now) this proposal does not evade the Enlightenment Problem. Consider again Lois's utterance of (2), in a conversation with Miles. Unless Lois is enlightened, she will have no reason to suppose that anything other than individuals are relevant to her utterance. She will not, then, intend to be interpreted as communicating anything about modes of presentation or aspects. So she won't assert anything like (2F) unless she is enlightened. Moreover, asserting (2F) would require that she at least take her audience to be enlightened as well—otherwise she would not think that they could work (2F) out as an immediate consequence of her utterance.[13] Yet Lois's enlightenment or lack thereof does not seem to have an impact on the intuition that her utterance of (2) is true. As we have seen in earlier chapters, the intuition that (2) is true remains even after we have been told that Lois and her audience are unenlightened. This intuition does not track the speaker's enlightenment as it would need to if it were to be explained in terms of assertion—which depends (in part) upon at least the speaker's state of mind.

One might attempt a response on the Soamesian's behalf: Soames only requires that asserted propositions be intended *in normal cases*. If we understand Lois as not knowing the meaning of (2), then her utterance will not be a normal one—she could assert (2F) without intending to do so. But it just seems wrong and question-begging to insist that Lois fails to know the meaning of (2). She seems like a competent speaker of the language and competent user of 'Superman' and 'Clark Kent'. To count anyone who is not aware of a double life as not knowing the meaning of a sentence about the person who leads that life seems a drastic and implausible move.[14]

---

[13] It may also be that the audience needs to be enlightened, so that they can in fact get to (2F) as an immediate inference. This is not clear from Soames's discussion.

[14] One can, however, make this move, insisting that our intuitions about this case are to be explained as due to an asserted proposition that plays no role at all in the mental lives of conversational participants—since they do not know the meaning of the sentence uttered. This will have many features in common with the proposal discussed in section 5.4 of this chapter, and it will suffer from the same problems. Alternatively, one might maintain that aspect-sensitive propositions may be asserted by utterances of simple sentences even when speakers clearly do not intend to convey these propositions—and even though they *do* understand the sentences that they utter. For this interpretation, one needs to understand non-standard cases, for Soames, as somehow including these. I am not entirely clear on what non-question-begging criterion could do this. However, if one adopts this interpretation then Soames has available to him the view that aspect-sensitive propositions really are asserted in the relevant cases—even though these propositions are not intended by the speakers. Again, this will suffer from much the same problems as the view discussed in section 5.4 of this chapter.

5.3 SOME DIAGNOSIS

The Enlightenment Problem is quite clearly not just a problem for theories that focus exclusively on what is semantically expressed and what is implicated. Views based on Bach's and Soames's taxonomies fare no better than those based on (EOI). Moreover, they seemed to fail for related reasons: there are cases—like the Lois and Miles case—in which our intuitions do not correspond to any proposition that fits their taxonomies. For Soames, the semantic content of Lois's utterance of (2) did not accord with our intuitions; and there was no proposition according to our intuitions that might have been asserted or implicated by Lois's utterance. For Bach, there was no proposition corresponding to our intuitions that might have been expressed, implicated, or implicited by Lois's utterance.

Despite the differences in semantic and pragmatic frameworks, and the differences in terminology, the failures of Soames's and Bach's accounts to offer a mechanism for explaining simple sentence intuitions was due to a common feature: there is no proposition Lois might have meant whose truth conditions match those indicated by our intuitions about Lois's utterance of (2). This fact played a role in the failures of the accounts we surveyed in Chapters 2 and 3 as well. Other factors that played a role: there was no such intuition-matching proposition that Lois would have expected her audience to work out; there was no such intuition-matching proposition that Lois's audience *did* work out; there was no such intuition-matching proposition that Lois's audience *could* work out. In short, there was no intuition-matching proposition that could have played the right sort of role in the conversational participants' minds.

The sensible question at this point, it seems to me, is why there has been so much concern over the role that an intuition-matching proposition might play in *conversational participants'* states of mind. Our intuitions, after all, are *ours*. It is a fact about my mental life that I have some intuition *i*. It is a fact about your mental life that you have some intuition *j*. An explanation of how I come to have intuition *i*, then, should turn on facts about my mental life; and an explanation of how you come to have intuition *j* should turn on facts about your mental life. So why should it be that the states of mind of conversational participants restrict what explanations are available for *my* intuitions? Prima facie, there would seem to be no good reason.

5.4 MOVING FURTHER FROM (EOI)

If these reflections are right, then the way to solve the enlightenment problem may be to focus on the psychological processes of those whose intuitions are being explained. This suggests the need for a new sort of account—one on which explanations of *our* intuitions turn only on claims about *our* states of mind.

It is important to appreciate what a large switch this is from traditional thinking about semantics. It has for some time now been clear that there are many sorts of utterances whose truth conditions seem, intuitively, to vary with context. A natural first move is to try to accommodate these intuitions in semantics, by offering a semantic theory on which truth conditions actually do vary with context. The elements which can effect such contextual variation are hotly debated: some insist that the only legitimate factors are 'objective' ones such as speaker, location, and time; others want to widen contextually relevant factors to include factors like speaker intentions and audience interests. (Accounts of simple sentences that make use of a contextually varying semantics are of this latter sort.) Another way of coping with contextually varying intuitions is, of course, to explain them away. When this is done, pragmatic notions like implicature (or, as we've seen implici*t*ure or assertion) are often invoked. Sometimes, however, explanations are not this specific—they discuss how conversational participants' perspectives might affect their intuitions without utilising such notions. Always, however, the explanations are in terms of the conversational participants' perspectives.

It seems to me that this is a mistake. The states of mind of conversational participants are the logical place to look for explanations of the intuitions of conversational participants. But it is far from obvious that they are the logical place to look for explanations of *our* intuitions. And if what I have argued thus far is right, our intuitions (about simple sentences, at least) *cannot* be explained by looking to the states of mind of conversational participants—even if we do look beyond what is expressed or implicated. And this means that the standard ways of thinking about contextually varying intuitions must be rejected. We must not confine ourselves to considerations that are available or salient to conversational participants—looking at their perspectives may well be a mistake when it is not their intuitions that we are seeking to explain.

Now we have a new place to look for an explanation of our intuitions about simple sentences: our states of mind. Our intuitions might err due to facts about our own psychology, rather than facts about conversational participants' psychology. This thought allows us to take seriously the idea that our intuitions might be explained by our grasp of some proposition that the conversational participants simply wouldn't entertain. We need no longer rule out an explanation that (for example) utilises aspect-sensitive propositions that unenlightened conversational participants would not consider: our intuitions might well be due to such a proposition. In the remainder of this chapter, I suggest an explanation that makes use of just such intuition-matching propositions. This explanation fares better than ones that are constrained by the perspectives of conversational participants. Nonetheless, it faces serious difficulties. In particular, it fails to evade the Aspect Problem (discussed in Chapters 2 and 3). But, in the following chapter, I suggest a different sort of story, one that is both immune to these problems and independently plausible.

5.4.1 A first try—we grasp intuition-matching propositions

This account takes its inspiration from the thought that an intuition-matching proposition need not be expressed, implicited, implicated, asserted, meant, or understood by the audience in order to play a role in explaining my intuitions. As long as *I* grasp that proposition, and as long as my intuitions can be explained as arising from that proposition, there is no reason to care about what role it plays in the mental lives of others—such as the conversational participants.

This sort of account could explain errors in our intuitions as due to aspect-sensitive propositions that we entertain, without making any commitments at all about the role these propositions play in the mental lives of conversational participants. According to this account, then, simple sentences do not express aspect-sensitive propositions. The names occurring in them have their referents as sole semantic contribution. Thus, utterances of (2) and (2*) express the same proposition and have the same truth value (indeed also the same truth conditions—the same truth values when evaluated at other possible worlds).

(2) Superman leaps more tall buildings than Clark Kent.
(2*) Superman leaps more tall buildings than Superman.

On this account, aspect-sensitive propositions make a difference to our intuitions. The propositions that make this difference, however, need not play any particular role in the mental lives of those having the conversation we are considering. For example, when we evaluate sentence (2) we are led astray by entertaining a proposition like that expressed by (2M).

(2) Superman leaps more tall buildings than Clark Kent.
(2M) Superman's 'Superman'-aspect leaps more tall buildings than Superman's 'Clark Kent'-aspect.

Because (2M) could be true, it wrongly seems to us that (2) could be true. This explanation has a familiar feel to it. As far as our psychology goes, it is just like the implicature explanations that we have already examined and dismissed (or like the impliciture story, or like the assertion story): the idea is that our truth-conditional intuitions are led astray by our entertaining some proposition other than the one expressed by the sentence—and that this other proposition has just the truth conditions indicated by our intuitions. The difference comes from the fact that this explanation, unlike the others, confines itself to claims about *our* psychology. It makes no claim that the other proposition we entertain—(2M), in the current example—has any kind of status at all for the conversational participants—that (2M) is implicated, that the speaker means (2M), that the speaker asserts (2M), or that the audience grasps (2M). These sorts of claims, as we have seen, are the ones that get theorists into trouble in explaining our intuitions—conversational participants' states of mind may change without our intuitions changing. This mismatch between our states of mind and conversational participants' states of mind is what produces the Enlightenment Problem. So the idea behind this account is to abandon these problematic commitments regarding the intuition-matching aspect-sensitive proposition—while keeping the claim that it is responsible for our intuitions. And this seems a promising strategy: the propositions needed to explain our intuitions are ones only the enlightened are likely to grasp, but we *are* enlightened. So problems like those that come from considering the states of mind of unenlightened conversational participants will simply not arise.

5.4.2 Why entertain aspect-sensitive propositions?

The first problem for this account emerges when we consider the question of why it is that we might be entertaining these aspect-sensitive propositions and getting confused by them—after all, they are neither expressed nor implicated. How do we come to think about them, and to be confused by them?

One might suppose that we come to think about an aspect-sensitive proposition when we encounter (2) simply because we are aware that (2) cannot express a truth.

(2) Superman leaps more tall buildings than Clark Kent.

Trying to be charitable to whoever has uttered (2), we move to thinking of some related proposition that could be true. We arrive, perhaps, at something like the aspect-sensitive (2M).

(2M) Superman's 'Superman'-aspect leaps more tall buildings than Superman's 'Clark Kent'-aspect.

After this charitable effort, we get confused and think that (2) is true, because now we are thinking about (2M). This story, however, is rather strange. After all, on this story the reason that we start considering aspect-sensitive propositions is that we think (2) is false. Why should considering (2M) make us change our mind about this? We might well conclude that the utterer of (2) wanted to convey what's expressed by (2M), but once we've judged that (2) is false it is difficult to see how anything about (2M) would persuade us otherwise. This story is especially poor at explaining the persistent intuitions of (2)'s truth that many people experience, and on which some base semantic theories. This explanation does well at explaining how people who *really* think (2) is false might understand the utterances of those who think it is true. But it does nothing to explain why it is that enlightened people may think—either briefly or enduringly—that (2) is true.

An alternative story is only marginally better. On this story, when we encounter an utterance of (2) our initial intuition is one of truth. Then we realise that (2) can't be true. Now the charitable routine kicks in again, and we generate (2M) in order to be generous to the person who uttered (2). The fact (2M) is true—which accords with our initial intuition—adds to the confusion generated by considering (2M), and we therefore take (2) to be true. This may be a reasonable story of how we might come, eventually, to consider an aspect-sensitive proposition. However, it is decidedly a non-starter as an explanation for the initial intuition that (2) is true—this intuition, our main subject matter, isn't addressed at all.

What these two failed efforts show is that we need a story on which we consider (2M) as soon as we encounter (2). Only such a story can explain the initial intuition that (2) is true. On such a story, we don't need to go through any reasoning process like those suggested above—because we *always* entertain aspect-sensitive propositions when we encounter sentences involving names of those that we know to live double-lives. This story could be motivated by the fact that we need to have a way to keep track of those leading 'double lives'. Although sometimes we want to reflect on the fact that one individual both writes for the *Daily Planet* and stops speeding trains/bullets, much of the time such reflection would only confuse us. After all, we need to be able to think sensibly about the thoughts of those who don't realise that 'Superman' and 'Clark Kent' co-refer, and to remember which things will be done in which outfit. Much of the time, then, it will be useful to us to focus not on the individual, but on his separate aspects. We get in the habit, then, of entertaining aspect-sensitive propositions on a regular basis. This habit leads us into trouble, as our focus on these aspect-sensitive propositions *sometimes* causes us to give the wrong verdicts on the truth of utterances of sentences like (2).

But is this a plausible story? It seems to me that it isn't: although this account has a certain superficial appeal, it starts to look far less likely when we give some thought to what is involved in entertaining propositions. Entertaining a proposition seems as though it must involve, at a minimum, representing that proposition in some way and considering it. After all, entertaining a proposition is a conscious activity of consideration. While it makes intuitive sense to suppose that we might tacitly *believe* a proposition—that is, believe it without consciously representing it—it just doesn't make sense to speak of 'tacit *entertaining*'. The view we are considering, then, is one on which our intuitions about (2) are explained by the fact that whenever we encounter a sentence like (2) we consciously entertain a representation corresponding to the proposition expressed by something like (2M) or (2F):

(2M) Superman's Superman-aspect leaps more tall buildings than Superman's Clark-aspect.
(2F) Superman, so-personified, leaps more tall buildings than Clark, so-personified.

What might this representation be? Let's start by assuming that the representation will be a sentence, and see what sort of sentence it would need to be. It can't be sentence (2), even though Moore would take

(2) to express something like (2M) and Forbes would take it to express something like (2F). It can't be (2) because on the view under discussion (though not on Forbes's and Moore's views), (2) simply expresses a *false* proposition about the individual Superman/Clark. (2M) and (2F), however, both express aspect-sensitive propositions whose entertainment is meant to explain the intuition that (2) is *true*.

Could it be that we automatically entertain a sentence like (2M) or (2F) when we encounter a sentence like (2)? This seems unlikely. The terminology involved in (2M) and (2F) is awkward and technical to the ordinary speaker, and requires substantial explanation for even semantic theorists to grasp. (Think, for example, of the important differences between Moore's aspects—things that can walk and talk—and Forbes, which are simply ways for individuals to be. For more on these differences, see the discussion in Chapter 2). The thought that anyone automatically entertains a sentence like (2M) or (2F) when they encounter (2) is highly implausible.[15]

However, there are more commonsensical variants, perhaps, of (2M) and (2F). As Forbes and Moore have pointed out, it *does* come pretty naturally to us to think and talk about roles that people play. It is more plausible to suppose that we might readily entertain something like (2R) than that we might readily entertain something like (2M) or (2F):

(2R) Superman, playing his Superman-role,[16] leaps more tall buildings than Clark, in his Clark-role.[17]

Moreover, it is (of course) not just *sentences* that we entertain, but also other sorts of representations. It is not implausible at all to suppose that we sometimes entertain propositions about roles, via *some* sort of mental representation.

It is substantially less plausible, though, that we do this *whenever* we encounter a sentence like (2), or even most of the times that we do. It

---

[15] It gets more implausible if we think about what's *really* involved. For Forbes, *so-personified* amounts to *personified in the so-labelled way*. The idea that we're really regularly thinking about labels for modes of personification just seems introspectively wrong. However, it's not the case that every aspect-sensitive view would need to make use of labelling of this sort, so I ignore it in the text above.

[16] I am using 'Superman-role' as a name for the role associated with the name 'Superman', and 'Clark-role' for the role associated with 'Clark Kent'.

[17] It is perhaps worth noting that it seems to me far more difficult to arrive at a commonsense understanding of Moore-type aspects. Roles, understood commonsensically, are things that *get played*, not things that can fly, leap buildings, and walk down the street. I'm not sure that we have any sort of ordinary notion corresponding to aspects, which can do all these things.

just doesn't seem right, introspectively, to suppose that when we encounter something like (2)—which doesn't express an aspect-sensitive proposition, we immediately conjure up for ourselves some representation of an aspect-sensitive proposition, and our entertainment of *this* proposition is what leads us to deem (2) false.[18] Serious consideration of what is involved in entertaining a proposition seems, then, to cast doubt upon this alternative matching-proposition story. However, these considerations are not decisive—introspection is a poor guide to what actually goes on in psychological processing. Further difficulties emerge, however, when we turn our attention back to the Aspect Problem.

5.4.3 Which aspect-sensitive propositions? The Aspect Problem revisited

The last chapter and most of this one have focused on the Enlightenment Problem—on the assumptions that give rise to this problem, and on what is needed to avoid it. The Enlightenment Problem has helped us to see that it is a mistake to insist that our intuitions must be explained by something that is dependent on the states of mind of conversational participants, rather than on our states of mind. An account that avoids this sort of dependence is able to avoid the Enlightenment Problem. It doesn't seem to me, then, that the Enlightenment Problem arises for the sort of account we are currently considering.

However, we have by no means left all problems behind. In our detailed consideration of the Enlightenment Problem, we turned our attention away from the Aspect Problem. I now want to turn back to it. The Aspect Problem, recall, was that of explaining what aspects and modes of personification are, how we manage to talk about them, and what the intuition-matching propositions involving them are.

We have already raised some worries about the first bit of the Aspect Problem: what the aspects or modes of personification this account draws on are. Are they Moorean aspects? Forbesian modes of personification? There seems no good way to settle this. Indeed, it seems that the only plausible version of the current account will have it that the propositions responsible for the truth-conditional intuitions of the enlightened involve neither of these—instead, they involve some

---

[18] This sort of worry can also be raised about implicature explanations of our anti-substitution intuitions about simple sentences. It just doesn't feel right to suggest that we are automatically entertaining these additional, aspect-sensitive propositions.

commonsense notion of roles. This seems far more intuitive than to suppose that we actually regularly entertain propositions involving Moore's or Forbes's aspects or modes, but is it a satisfactory answer? It seems far more like an avoidance of the question than an answer to it. We really don't know what these things are.

We can begin to see how unsatisfactory an answer it is when we turn to the third portion of the Aspect Problem—what the aspect-involving propositions are—and remember the work that we want these propositions to do. The idea behind the current account is that our anti-substitution intuitions are to be explained as arising not from what is expressed by utterances of simple sentences but instead from aspect-sensitive propositions that we happen to entertain as we are considering these utterances. These propositions, then, must have truth conditions matching our truth-conditional intuitions. This means we need to know more—we need to know what counts as playing the commonsense 'Superman'-role. Very quickly, all the familiar problems will arise—who will decide this? What if conversational participants disagree? What about when he's wearing the capeless outfit? And so on . . . [19] The Aspect Problem, then, is alive and well for our current attempted account.

In this chapter, we have seen that it is possible to avoid the Enlightenment Problem. We can do this by invoking intuition-matching propositions that are entertained by those whose intuitions are at stake, whether or not they play any particular role in the mental lives of conversational participants. But these all-important propositions will still make use of something like aspects or modes of personification. And this means that the Aspect Problem remains. In the next chapter, we abandon the quest for intuition-matching propositions, and we see that we are finally able to leave the Aspect Problem behind as well.

---

[19] I will not bore the reader by rehearsing these examples in detail again. They can be found at §2.2.2 and §3.1.2.1.

6

Beyond Matching Propositions

So far, we've seen that the problem posed by simple sentences is not one that is easily solved by way of traditional methods. Efforts to find a semantic theory that yields truth conditions in accord with our intuitions have failed, as (so far) have efforts to explain away the intuitions. The intuitions cannot be explained as arising from implicated, asserted, implicited or expressed propositions whose truth conditions match the intuitions. Nor do there seem to be any other such intuition-matching propositions that would be available in the right ways to conversational participants in all cases. One key reason for this has been, of course, the Enlightenment Problem. In the last chapter, I argued that it is a mistake to focus exclusively on conversational participants' states of mind: we should not assume that *our* intuitions are to be explained as resulting from a proposition that plays some particular role in the mental lives of conversational participants.

Once we abandon this assumption, we can successfully evade the Enlightenment Problem. With this in mind, I have begun to explore instead the possibility that incorrect intuitions might be explained with reference to the states of mind of those having the intuitions, rather than the conversational participants. At the end of the last chapter, we explored a possible account on which truth-conditional intuitions are to be explained as arising simply from some proposition entertained by the person having the intuitions—without any reference to the role this proposition plays in the lives of conversational participants. This account, however, seemed to require the use of something like Moore's aspects or Forbes's modes of personification. And doing so means that the Aspect Problem remains. Any account that makes use of these entities needs to offer a satisfying story about what these entities are, how we talk and think about them, and the truth conditions of the propositions that involve them.

But can the use of aspect-like entities be avoided? In this chapter, I argue that it can be. We can avoid the need for aspects if we abandon the quest for intuition-matching propositions. If we can find a way to explain mistaken intuitions as arising from something other than the entertainment of intuition-matching propositions, we have no need for aspects in our explanation of simple sentence intuitions.

This chapter sketches an approach that takes just this form.[1] I argue that such an approach fits well with—and indeed is suggested by—certain independently plausible and widely accepted views regarding representation and cognitive organization. Given the naturalness and plausibility of this approach, and its lack of tendentious theoretical commitments, there seems to me good reason to suppose that we can and should take seriously explanations of this sort. I do not, however, claim to establish that it is correct. My goal is more modest: to show that there is room for such an approach, and to show how it might be supported by empirical evidence (some of which already exists and some of which does not).

6.1 PROPOSITIONS, WAYS OF GRASPING PROPOSITIONS

Let's start with a basic question: what goes on, cognitively speaking, when we encounter sentences like (1) and (1*) and evaluate them for truth value?

(1) Clark Kent went into the phone booth and Superman came out.
(1*) Superman went into the phone booth and Clark Kent came out.

The answer to this question is not a simple one. Many, many things can happen. There are, for example, many sorts of things that can go wrong, as we have already seen. We might misread or mishear, or we might focus on what the sentences implicate rather than on what they express. We might, for some other reason, entertain some proposition(s) that simply aren't expressed by the sentences. But we have already seen that mistakes like these cannot explain all of the cases that we need to explain—even though, assuredly, they can explain some of them. Let us focus, however, on cases where none of these mistakes take place. Our question now is what happens in such cases.

---

[1] This approach is a development of that suggested in Braun and Saul (2002).

On any remotely plausible view, different things go on in our heads when we encounter these different sentences. One way of capturing these differences—broadly speaking, the Fregean way—is to maintain that we entertain different propositions. Another way—broadly speaking, the Millian way—is to claim that we entertain the same proposition but that we represent it to ourselves in different ways.[2] These differences alone, of course, do not explain why we might take (1) to be true and (1*) to be false, in the same context. As we saw quite early on, both the traditional Millian and the traditional Fregean would assign these sentences the same truth value. And, if we know that (2) is true, both the Millian and the Fregean will struggle to explain why it is that we fail to realize that (1) and (1*) must take the same truth value—why we are willing to assign them different truth values.

(2) Superman is Clark Kent.

For the Fregean, the difficulty is that the proposition expressed by (1) and the proposition expressed by (2) together entail—via a very simple inference—the truth of the proposition expressed by (1*). If a speaker believes that (1) and (2) are true—and possesses basic logical competence—how can she possibly fail to believe that (1*) is true?

For the Millian, the problem at first seems even worse: after all, the Millian claims that (1) and (1*) express the very same proposition. But the Millian maintains that a speaker may represent one and the same proposition to herself in different ways without realizing that both representations are of the same proposition. So the fact that (1) and (1*) express the same proposition is not in itself a problem. The problem lies in the fact that this proposition, and that expressed by (2), are very likely to be represented in ways that seem as though they should make it obvious that (1) and (1*) cannot take different truth values. Take the case of Frieda, for example, who thinks (1) is true and (1*) is false, despite accepting (2). One way that Frieda might present these propositions to herself is via the sentences (1), (1*), and (2), or mental analogues of them. If she does this, it is clear that the inference from (1) to (1*) should be a very obvious one for her, given her beliefs. Yet Frieda's intuitions persist.

These difficulties prompted theorists like Forbes, Moore, and Pitt to propose novel semantic theories on which (1) and (1*) not only express

---

[2] As noted earlier, not all Millians make use of ways of believing (see, for example Thau 2002). For objections to Millianism that does not make use of ways of believing, see Braun (2002).

different propositions, but propositions with different truth values. But we have seen that these theories face serious problems. Now my goal is to take a new look at the resources available to those who don't make this move—that is, those who want to deny that (1) and (1*) can differ in truth value.

6.2 FAILURE TO REFLECT ON IDENTITY

The first thing to recall about the human mind is that we don't automatically make all the inferences that we can, even if when these inferences are very easy. For example, upon being told by a reliable informant that dinner is ready, I don't infer that either dinner is ready or Kevin Costner is President—or that dinner is ready and two plus two is four. We make inferences when we have some reason to do so. Among other things, we do not automatically consult our pre-existing beliefs every time that we add a new one, in order to see what inferences we can draw. One who encounters and accepts (1), then, will not necessarily reflect upon her background belief expressed by (2). If she does not do this, it will be no surprise that she would fail to realize that (1*) must be true. An enlightened person who judges that (1) is true while (1*) isn't is perhaps not as hard to explain as one might have supposed: failure to reflect on Superman's double life may be perfectly sufficient for some cases.

But this reply is a bit too quick. It is far more likely that one who encounters (1) will consider the claim expressed by (2) than it is that one who is told that dinner is ready will reflect upon Kevin Costner and the presidency. Many of the inferences we don't draw—like the Kevin Costner one—would require us to reflect on matters that are simply *irrelevant* to our current interests. We can easily see, then, why we fail to engage in such reflections. This is just not so in the case of a speaker who encounters (1) and fails to consider the identity captured in (2). After all, (2) not only contains both names that occur in (1)—it asserts the identity. Moreover, a sentence about the transition point should be one that calls attention to Superman's double life. How could a claim about this double life possibly be said to be irrelevant? Since it is so clearly relevant, the analogy to non-inferences like the Kevin Costner one does not get us very far in explaining *why* speakers might fail to infer from (1) to (1*). And that is what we need to explain.

What we need to explain now is why it is that one might entertain the proposition expressed by (1) without reflecting on Superman's double life in such a way as to infer that (1*) must take the same truth value as (1). One possible answer lies in the way that we store information about individuals, particularly when we are given more than one term that refers to a single individual.

6.3 SOME EXPERIMENTAL RESULTS

Somewhat surprisingly, there has not been much psychological research on how people process and store information about an individual who is known under more than one label (and none that I can find about individuals known under more than one *name*). However, John Anderson and Reid Hastie (Anderson 1977, Anderson and Hastie 1974) performed some experiments in the 1970s to discover how people store information about an individual when some of that information is presented under a name and other information under a description. They also studied how knowledge that the name and description co-refer affects the way information is stored. I take these experiments to show a very strong tendency to separate information learned under one label from information learned under another—even when the labels are known to co-refer. I argue that such separate storage gives us a way to explain anti-substitution intuitions about simple sentences.

Anderson and Hastie's experiments, in broadest outline, consist of three phases, whose order is sometimes varied. (My division into phases is slightly different from theirs, because some of the details of their experiments are not relevant to the discussion here. I am also using different names for the phases.)

- *Identity Learning:* During this phase subjects are taught that certain pairs of names and descriptions are co-referential—e.g. they are taught that 'James Bartlett is the lawyer' is true. Subjects are drilled and tested on the identities and not allowed to proceed to later phases until they have shown sufficient facility with the identities.

- *Other Learning:* During this phase subjects are taught some facts about the individuals whose names and descriptions are involved in the Identity Learning phase—e.g. they are taught 'James Bartlett rescued the kitten'.

- *Verification:* During this phase subjects are asked to give truth values for three kinds of claims—(a) those they were explicitly taught in the Other Learning phase; (b) those that are inferable from these combined with the identities learned at the Identity Learning phase; and (c) claims which fit neither of these categories. Subjects are told to count a claim as true if it follows from those they have learned, and false otherwise.

A key portion of Anderson and Hastie's experiments involves comparing the speed and accuracy of subject responses when the order of these phases is varied. In the 'Before' conditions, Identity Learning precedes Other Learning, while in the 'After' conditions the order of these phases is reversed.

In the After conditions, subjects were substantially slower to verify (assign a truth value to) statements that required them to infer from a learned identity and other learned sentence[3] than to verify sentences that they had already seen. They were also more prone to error about such statements. That is (using the examples from the description above), they were less good at verifying 'The lawyer rescued the kitten' (which they had not seen before) than 'James Bartlett rescued the kitten' (which they had seen before). Anderson explains this data by putting forward a model on which subjects who learn phrases like 'James Bartlett' and 'the lawyer' set up mental representations which involve 'nodes' representing individuals, to which information like *rescued the kitten*,[4] and labels like 'James Bartlett' or 'the lawyer', are then attached. When they learn of the identity between what they previously took to be separate individuals, they set up a link between the two nodes, and they begin a process of transferring all the information to a single node, by choosing one node to copy it to and abandoning the other. However, this process is far from immediate, so time-consuming inferences are required to verify sentences like 'The lawyer rescued the kitten'.

It might seem that the data described above could be fully explained by the fact that subjects are quicker to recognize a sentence they have seen recently than one that they have not seen before. This could be taken as evidence that we store at least some information by remembering sentences that we encounter. There would be no need, then, to suggest that we store the information about James Bartlett at two different

---

[3] I use 'learned sentence' to refer to a sentence that subjects encountered in the Other Learning phase of the experiments.

[4] Exactly how this information is represented does not matter for our purposes here.

nodes. But there is more data that is not so easily explained this way. This data concerns the Before condition (in which Identity Learning precedes Other Learning) and different versions of the Identity Learning phase. It turns out that the exact nature of the Identity Learning phase is very important. If the Identity Learning phase includes drawings of individuals, and takes place before the Other Learning phase, subjects are not appreciably slower to verify inferred sentences than ones that they learned during Other Learning. For example, imagine subjects who have been taught, with drawings, that James Bartlett is the lawyer. (That is, when told that James Bartlett is the lawyer, subjects are also presented with sketches of the individual under discussion.) These subjects are then told 'James Bartlett rescued the kitten'. Later, they are asked to verify the truth of either 'James Bartlett rescued the kitten' or 'the lawyer rescued the kitten'. Their responses will be pretty much equally speedy and accurate in both cases. This shows that it is not merely memory for sentences already encountered that is doing the work. It really does look like subjects can either store the 'James Bartlett' and 'the lawyer' information together or not. If they store it together—as they seem to do when they learn the identity first, with drawings, then they don't need to make an additional inference that leads to delays and errors.

Importantly, however, if the Identity Learning phase does not include drawings, subjects are just as slow and inaccurate in their verifications in the Before condition as they are in the After condition. Anderson (1977) taught subjects the identities without drawings, and drilled them extensively on the identities before they proceeded to later phases of the experiments (not allowing them to proceed until they showed that they had learned the identities). In his experiments, however, subjects who learned the identities in this way in the Before condition exhibited errors and lag times of roughly the same sort as those who learned the identities *after* learning the other information. In these later experiments, subjects have no obvious reason to set up separate nodes associated with the name and the description, and to attach information to just one of these nodes—they know from the start that both refer to the same individual. And yet, Anderson argues, they appear to be setting up separate nodes and noting connections between them, rather than simply setting up a single node.

These experiments seem to me to show a tendency to store information learned under different labels separately—even when there is no good reason to do so. It makes a great deal of sense that subjects in the After condition would have a tendency to store information separately.

After all, when they went through the Other Learning phase, they did not yet know the name and description to be co-referential. But these are not the only subjects to show this tendency. The experiments in which the Identity Learning phase does not include drawings show that even when subjects are aware of the identity right from the start, they may *still* set up separate nodes for the name and description—which they know to co-refer. Importantly, these subjects learn the identities just as fully as those who are shown the drawings. (They do not proceed to the next phase of the experiment until they have done so.) Yet, nonetheless, they show a tendency to store the information learned under the name separately from the information learned under the description. I take this to show that we have a strong tendency to store such information separately, one that is difficult to overcome.

Before I can argue this, however, I need to say something about an alternative hypothesis. This alternative hypothesis, suggested by Anderson, is that subjects who did not see the drawings may have suffered from a sort of confusion about whether the learned identities should be taken into account at later stages of the experiment. At the identity-learning phase, subjects learn that James Bartlett is the lawyer and they clearly do understand this fact and retain it well enough to succeed at the drills. In the Other learning phase, they are told things like 'the lawyer drank the wine'. Finally, they are asked to verify statements like 'James Bartlett drank the wine'. Anderson notes that expressions like 'the lawyer' can be used to pick out more than one individual, and that subjects in the Other learning phase might not realize that 'the lawyer' is still meant to pick out James Bartlett. This uncertainty could lead them to set up a separate node for 'the lawyer', and cause delays and errors in the verification phase.

Anderson's suggestion would pose problems for the gloss I would like to put on the experiments: if he is right, then subjects who set up separate nodes for 'James Bartlett' and 'the lawyer' are doing so because—in the Other Learning phase—they are genuinely unsure about the identity. It does not look, then, like there is simply a tendency to segregate information about a single individual that is learned under two labels. But this hypothesis can't explain the data. There is absolutely no reason that exposure to drawings at the *Identity* Learning phase should make subjects at the *Other* Learning phase any more certain that 'the lawyer' still picks out the same person—the drawings could only do this if they were presented at the Other Learning phase as well. They were not. Since the drawings *do* cause subjects to integrate the information from the two labels, the phenomena can't be explained in terms of uncertainty about the identity.[5]

There are many things that these experiments do not show. To cite just two: They do not show, directly, anything at all about how subjects process information learned under different but co-referential *names*—they concern only co-referential name/*description* pairs. They also do not show what happens when subjects are asked the truth values of pairs of sentences obtained by substitution of co-referential phrases, as in (3) and (3*).

(3) The lawyer rescued the kitten.
(3*) James Bartlett rescued the kitten.

In addition, these experiments seem to show that subjects *do* begin a process of integrating information from the different labels, even though this process is not immediate. It turns out, for example that as further questions are asked response times shorten and error rates diminish. It looks, then, like subjects *do* eventually integrate the information. It might seem, then, that these experiments do not show much that will help me to formulate an explanation of intuitions about simple sentences (and that they may even hurt).

I think, however, that Anderson's experiments tell us a great deal that is very relevant to simple sentence intuitions, and helpful to the explanation that I will offer in this chapter. Here are just a few of the things that they tell us: most obviously, they tell us that bits of information believed to be about a single individual may nonetheless be stored separately, even if we learn the identity before we learn anything else about the individual. They show that it may take some effort to integrate this information. Finally, they tell us that this can happen even in cases—unlike double life cases—in which subjects have been given no good reason to segregate the information. These facts, I will suggest, can help us to understand intuitions about simple sentences.

A terminological note: as I discuss the applications of Anderson's work to simple sentences, I will often write in terms of his preferred

---

[5] According to Anderson's (1977) model, the name and description are initially attached to the same node in the Before Condition. It is only at the Other Learning phase (when identities are taught without drawings) that a new node is set up, which his results seem to indicate tends to be attached to the description. In the before Condition, then, the description, then is attached to both nodes while the name is attached to only one. This explains the fact that Anderson finds time lags in this condition for inferences to sentences containing names, but not those containing descriptions. For more on this, see Anderson (1977: 435).

cognitive metaphors[6]—nodes and attachments to nodes. Nothing I say, however, depends on this. All that matters to me here is the idea of segregating information known to be about a single individual but learned under different labels. This could just as well be explained in terms of many philosophers' favourite metaphor—belief and entertainment boxes, subdivided into folders labelled by names or descriptions. I am not suggesting here that there are no differences between these models, or even that there are no significant differences. However, I don't think that these differences matter for current purposes.

6.4 STORING SUPERMAN AND CLARK INFORMATION[7]

My first suggestion will be that we store *Superman* information separately from *Clark* information. This storage claim needs a bit more explanation, and a bit more justification. One way that we might store *Superman* information separately from *Clark* information is that we might associate some information directly with one name and some with another. Another thought, however, based on Anderson's hypotheses, is that we set up two 'individual' nodes (nodes that would normally be seen as representing separate individuals), and that each node is associated both with various bits of information and with a name. With either of these models, we would also need to store somewhere the idea that 'Clark' and 'Superman' co-refer. We could do this by setting up a link between the *Superman* and *Clark* nodes, while still storing different bits of information at the different nodes. We could also do this simply by storing the identity sentence at each node and making inferences from it. (Note that we could also be said to store whole sentences or sentence-like representations in named folders.) It is not clear to me what substantive difference there is between any of these models for our current purposes. It is worth noting, however, that the linguistic element of the models is quite dispensable. It is convenient to think of the nodes as labelled by names, but they need not be. We could set up separate *Superman* and *Clark* nodes simply on the basis of witnessing some costume changes,

---

[6] I refer to these as metaphors. Alternatively, one might prefer to think of them as abstract functional descriptions.

[7] The account discussed here is a development of Braun and Saul (2002). Any errors introduced in this new version are wholly my responsibility, not David Braun's.

some furtiveness, and the differences in behaviour displayed when caped and when suited. And we could do all this even if we never learned any names. For current purposes, I will write of *Superman* nodes and *Clark* nodes (and *Superman* and *Clark* information/beliefs), meaning this formulation to be neutral between the various versions of the model discussed in this paragraph.

The thought that we may store *Superman* information separately from *Clark* information gains support from considering a disanalogy between Anderson's experiments and simple sentence cases. The subjects in Anderson's experiments had no good reason for keeping the information learned under the name 'John Smith' separate from that learned under the description 'the lawyer'. This is not at all the case when we consider double lives. To see this, consider the following bit of a Superman plot.

Clark is dancing with Lois at a party. A thug attempts to cut in and Clark reluctantly adheres to his role as weakling, stepping aside. Lois declares her intention to leave, in a huff. The thug is rude to her and she slaps him. Now the thug attempts to start a fight with Clark, who refuses. Lois leaves Clark, accusing him of spinelessness. Superman follows the thug, who kidnaps Lois. Superman rescues her and flies back to the city with her in his arms. Lois smiles at Superman, but she does not even speak to Clark the next day.

Now, let's imagine what it would be like not to keep the information learned under 'Clark' somehow separated from that learned under 'Superman'. One way of modelling this is to imagine a person with a single Superman/Clark node. Such a person would deposit a lot of information at this one node: danced with Lois, let thug cut in, refused to fight thug, followed thug, saved Lois from thug, smiled at by Lois, not spoken to by Lois the next day. This is clearly not the best way to recall the story—retrieving this information could lead to a great deal of confusion. Alternatively, we might imagine storing the summary as mental sentences, and instantly inferring from these mental sentences to those we get by substituting.

Clark is dancing with Lois at a party. *(So Superman is dancing with Lois at a party.)* A thug attempts to cut in and Clark reluctantly adheres to his role as weakling, stepping aside. *(So Superman reluctantly adheres to his role as weakling, stepping aside.)* Lois declares her intention to leave, in a huff. The thug is rude to her and she slaps him. Now the thug attempts to start a fight with Clark, who refuses. *(So now the thug attempts to start a fight with Superman, who refuses.)* Lois leaves Clark, accusing him of spinelessness. *(So Lois leaves Superman, accusing him of spinelessness.)* Superman follows the thug, who kidnaps Lois. *(So Clark follows the thug, who kidnaps Lois.)* Superman rescues her and flies back to the city with her in his arms. *(So Clark rescues her and flies back to the city with her in his arms.)* Lois smiles at Superman, but she does not even speak to Clark the next day. *(So Lois smiles at Clark, but she does not even speak to Superman the next day.)*

Whatever our preferred model for storage of information, it is clear that fully integrating information learned under 'Superman' and information learned under 'Clark' (whatever this comes to) is not a good strategy. It is very much in one's interests to keep these kinds of information separate—otherwise even recalling the plot of a comic book becomes difficult.

This little thought experiment helps to make it clear that we really can't afford to constantly infer from 'Clark' sentences to 'Superman' sentences (and vice versa). We have very good reason not to constantly reflect upon something like (2) and draw out the consequences—if we did, it would be much more difficult even to follow the plot of a comic book. In the case of double lives, like Superman/Clark, it would seem natural for us to go out of our way to *avoid* integrate information from the different nodes most of the time. It would make sense for our default to be keeping such information separate. The fact that such integration is not automatic even when we have no reason to avoid integrating—as in Anderson's experiments—helps to make plausible the thought that we might fail to integrate when we have very good reason not to.

Put in Anderson's preferred terms, the thought would be that when we have good reason to avoid copying information from one node to another, we *don't* begin a process of copying all the information over to a single node and abandoning the other one. Instead, we maintain both nodes and an awareness of the link between them. We *can* use this link to infer that information linked to one node could also be linked to the other, but we don't always do this. Importantly, we don't develop the habit of using the link to make such inferences—we may even develop the habit of not doing so.

Sometimes, of course, we do integrate our *Superman* and *Clark* beliefs. I am not at all claiming that we cannot integrate such information—obviously we can, and sometimes we do. We might do this, for example, if we are told the following story:

Clark got up at 8 and ate a huge plate of bacon and eggs, toast, pancakes, some cereal, and a left-over pizza from the night before. He left the house, went to the nearest phone booth, and emerged as Superman at 8.30. Lois happened to be walking by, and she invited him to have breakfast with her at a local diner. Is it likely that Superman was hungry enough to eat much with Lois?

To follow this story and reflect upon Superman's likely appetite we actually need to remember that Superman leads a double life. To answer the question above containing the name 'Superman', we need to consult information stored at the *Clark* node. We can do this: after all, we do know of a link between the *Superman* node and the *Clark* node. When we do this, we will retrieve the information *ate a huge breakfast*, and combine this with some real-world knowledge to arrive at the conclusion that the answer to the question is 'no'.[8]

But, as I have suggested, we don't always integrate our *Superman* beliefs and our *Clark* beliefs. One reason we might not do so is that we fail to reflect upon the *Superman/Clark* identity. This seems a fairly satisfying explanation of the initial intuition that (4) may be true:

(4) Superman leaps more tall buildings than Clark Kent does.

When deciding about (4)'s truth, we consult our relevant beliefs. Some of these are stored at the *Clark* node, and some at the *Superman* node. At the *Superman* node, we find information like *leaps tall buildings in a single bound;* at the Clark node, we find information like *sort of wimpy, doesn't do anything extraordinary,* and so on. At the *Superman* node, we may find images of a caped man flying over a building; and at the *Clark* node, we may find images of a man in a suit stumbling over his own shoelaces and looking highly incapable of leaping tall buildings. If we reflected on the identity, we could infer (for example) that the individual represented by the *Clark* node also leaps tall buildings in a single bound. This would make us far less likely to say that (4) is true. But we have good reason for—and a well-established habit of—not reflecting on the identity, and not making such inferences. So we don't do so. Hence, we take (4) to be true.

Similarly, it is fairly simple to explain the intuition that (4*) can't be true, when we consider it on its own.

(4*) Superman leaps more tall buildings than Superman does.

This intuition could result simply from the surface form of the sentence—which seems to describe an impossible state of affairs.[9] The

---

[8] A fan of mental sentences might describe this differently: We might think to ourselves, using mental sentences, 'Clark ate a huge breakfast not long ago'; then reflect on another mental sentence we take to be true, 'Clark is Superman'; infer to the mental sentence 'Superman ate a huge breakfast not long ago'; and, finally, consult our real-world knowledge to conclude that the answer to the question should be 'no'.

[9] That is, unless we've been led to view the two occurrences of 'Superman' as referring to different individuals—as might happen with 'Aristotle' in a comparison known to

intuition could also be taken to result from a consultation of the information at the 'Superman' node—*leaps more tall buildings than Superman* isn't there, and looking at what is stored at the node, we can't imagine it being there, or anything else that might support it.

But things get a little trickier when we are presented with (4) and (4*) together:

(4) Superman leaps more tall buildings than Clark Kent does.
(4*) Superman leaps more tall buildings than Superman does.

Presenting these sentences together—with the only difference being a single substitution—makes it likely that one will reflect on the double life, and doing so in an article or book on substitution puzzle cases all the more so. It also seems overwhelmingly likely that the reader of (1)—even before she is presented with (1*)—will reflect upon the double life.

(1) Clark Kent went into the phone booth and Superman came out.
(1*) Superman went into the phone booth and Clark Kent came out.

As I noted earlier, the double life is surely relevant to the phone booth scene—after all, we all know what goes on in the phone booth.[10] Reading a sentence like (1), alluding to the transition between the 'Clark' look and the 'Superman' look, can't help but remind us of Superman's double life. We need to explain, then, how it is that we might reflect upon the double life and *still* not integrate all the Superman and Clark beliefs, and infer that (1) and (1*), and (4) and (4*), must take the same truth value.

I think this demand can be met, and rather easily. Reflecting upon the double life does not mean making all the inferences that one can make from it. After all, Superman's double life plays an important role throughout the Superman stories, yet it is clear that readers of these stories—however aware they are of the double life—are not constantly inferring everything that the double life would allow them to infer. To make sense of this in Anderson's terms, all we need to posit is that one may be aware of the link between the *Superman* node and the *Clark* node without having any tendency to use the link to combine information from the two nodes. We have good reason not use the link in this way. Indeed, as we have seen, it seems perfectly sensible to suppose that we

---

be between the philosopher and the shipping magnate: 'Aristotle was not as good a businessman as Aristotle'.

[10] Well, in some sense we do. What happens to the suit, tie, shoes, etc. remains a mystery.

would establish strong habits, in double life cases, of not making all the relevant inferences.

Unfortunately, we do not have psychological experiments to directly support the sort of picture sketched above. What we do have is the knowledge that even when we know a name and a description to co-refer, we do not immediately or reliably integrate all the information that we have learned about the individual. This fact makes it reasonable to suppose that we might fail to immediately or reliably integrate all the information that we have learned under two different names. Moreover, the cases studied in experiments on names and descriptions are ones in which subjects had no good reason to keep separate the information learned under the name from the information learned under the description. The fact that they did so even under these circumstances makes it likely that there would be failures of integration—almost certainly many more such failures—when subjects have good reason not to integrate.

6.5 WHY DON'T ALL SUBJECTS INTEGRATE WHEN EXPLICITLY LED THROUGH THE INFERENCE?

We don't yet, however, have a full explanation of what goes on with simple sentence intuitions. For some of these intuitions persist even after speakers are told to reflect on the identity and invited to consider the inference from, say, (1) and (2) to (1*):

(1) Clark Kent went into the phone booth and Superman came out.
(2) Superman is Clark Kent.
(1*) Superman went into the phone booth and Clark Kent came out.

It is very clear, for example, that the anti-substitution intuitions persist for Graeme Forbes, Joe Moore, David Pitt and Stefano Predelli even after they have reflected upon these sentences and the inferences that they might make. The current story does not yet explain this. The current story insists that the inference is acceptable, and, more generally, that substitution of co-referential names in simple sentences cannot result in a change of truth value. Our tendency not to realize this has been explained, so far, by the suggestions that we store *Superman* and *Clark* information separately, and that—despite our knowledge that 'Superman is Clark' is true, we have a well-motivated and deeply ingrained habit of *not* always integrating *Superman* and *Clark* information. But we have already noted that sometimes we *do* make such inferences—as in the case where we are reflecting on Superman's appetite. It seems, then, inexplicable so far that people could fail to make the inference above even when they are invited to do so—given that the inference is correct, and that they have been led through it.

It is worth pausing for a moment to reflect on what I need to explain at this stage. I have already offered an explanation of our initial anti-substitution intuitions. Now my goal is to explain why these intuitions may persist, even as we are led through an inference that should (on my view) demonstrate that they are mistaken. That is, why it is that someone who is presented with (1) and (1*), and invited to reflect on a possible inference from (1) and (2) to (1*), might nonetheless refuse to make the inference. As it turns out, there are many reasons this might happen.

Failure to draw simple inferences is by no means a novelty: anyone who has taught critical thinking is very familiar with the phenomenon. This may well explain some failures to infer from (1) and (2) to (1*). But this surely cannot explain all cases, and the inference really is of a structure that should be obvious enough even to many of the weakest of critical thinking students.

A better explanation begins from the strength of the intuitions that (1) is true in the situation described and (1*) is false. Psychologists have found that people are reluctant to infer to conclusions that they take to be false, even if they are being asked about validity of inferences rather than about what is true (Oakhill, Johnson-Laird and Garnham 1989). Those who are convinced that (1) is true and (1*) false may well refuse to make the inference from (1) and (2) to (1*) even when explicitly invited to do so.

Why should subjects fail to infer to conclusions they take to be false? One possibility is that they may have greater confidence in their truth-conditional judgments than in their inference-making. Again, a lack of confidence about what follows from what is a familiar feature of critical thinking classes—and one that can certainly lead to errors in inference-making.

But those who have quite a bit of appropriate confidence in their logical acumen—Forbes, Pitt, Predelli, and Moore, for example—may have even stronger reasons to resist seemingly obvious inferences. They know, after all, that surface form is often misleading. Because of this knowledge, they may place more faith in their truth-conditional judgments than in the superficial validity of the inference or the apparently obvious truth of (2). This is an eminently reasonable thing for such people to do.

For some such people—e.g. Forbes, Moore, Pitt and Predelli—the next step is to offer semantic theories that vindicate their intuitions. This is why they have developed detailed and sophisticated semantic theories on which what looks to be a valid substitution inference may not be. But such theories are not necessary in order to maintain a reluctance to substitute: all that is needed is greater confidence in the truth-conditional intuitions that count against substitution than in the arguments for substitution. And, given just the knowledge that superficial form may be misleading, this confidence is perfectly reasonable. For those who have such confidence, no amount of pointing out the seemingly valid substitution inference will make substitution seem acceptable in cases where initial intuition counts against it. Hence, a strong and lasting resistance to resistance to substitution in such cases makes perfect sense.

A slightly more detailed look at Forbes, Moore, Pitt and Predelli is also revealing. One thing we notice is that Forbes, Moore and Predelli are clearly trying to account for different intuitions from those that Pitt aims to accommodate. (Though there are some similarities, of course.) All four would agree that (4) may at least sometimes be true.

(4) Superman leaps more tall buildings than Clark Kent does.

For Forbes and Moore, this is because in some contexts (4) expresses an aspect-sensitive proposition. In these contexts it will be true. Predelli agrees that (4) will only sometimes be true. For Pitt, (4) is always true: it always expresses a proposition about two alter-egos, one of whom leaps more tall buildings than the other. Pitt, then, unlike Forbes, Moore and Predelli, would never allow substitution in (4). Moreover, he takes this result to be perfectly intuitive.

A further difference: Forbes, Moore and Predelli maintain that in some contexts (5) will express a truth.

(5) Batman is more resistant to bullets than Bruce Wayne is.

Pitt, however, does not. For Pitt, 'Bruce Wayne' is the name of a primum ego, and 'Batman' the name of an alter ego. Since everything that is true of an alter ego is also true of a primum ego, (5) must take the same truth value as the obviously false (5*):

(5*) Bruce Wayne is more resistant to bullets than Bruce Wayne is.

Again, Pitt takes this result to be the intuitive one.

A good account of simple sentence intuitions should be able to explain variations in intuitions. The story developed in this chapter seems to me to have a great deal of room for individual variation. Some readers of Batman comic books will always think about the fact that the man under the mask is really Bruce Wayne (perhaps they even picture his face). Such readers will, perhaps, always integrate in the way suggested by Pitt's view. In Anderson's terms, they always copy any *Batman* beliefs to the *Bruce Wayne* node. They might, like Pitt, do this while at the same time not integrating in the other direction. If they don't always think of the Bat-suit when Bruce isn't wearing it, they may not copy all *Bruce Wayne* beliefs to the *Batman* node. But one might do all of this while treating the case of Superman very differently. One might well fail to integrate *Superman* and *Clark Kent* beliefs in the same way that one integrates *Batman* and *Bruce Wayne* beliefs. This could happen as a result of developed thoughts about primum and alter egos, but—more likely—such tendencies could also serve as the motivation for developing such views. A speaker with these tendencies will find a theory like Pitt's very natural.

In all likelihood, reflecting on and holding a view like Pitt's will also strengthen these tendencies, by providing *good reason* to integrate (some) Batman and Bruce Wayne beliefs. I have already suggested that pre-existing tendencies to segregate beliefs—like those Anderson observed—may be strengthened in cases (like Superman/Clark) where there is good reason to segregate. It is very plausible to suppose that having good reason to integrate beliefs would strengthen one's tendencies to do so. Explaining such a speaker requires building in slightly different tendencies from those needed for a speaker like Forbes, Predelli or Moore, but the basic cognitive architecture remains the same: *Superman* and *Clark* beliefs, and *Batman* and *Bruce Wayne* beliefs are stored separately, with individual variations regarding when (if ever) to integrate.

6.6 WHY DO SOME SUBJECTS INTEGRATE MORE EASILY?

A further sort of individual variation one might predict is that some people may integrate beliefs easily. Although these people may still store their *Superman* and *Clark* beliefs separately, they will be very willing to integrate these beliefs either when relevant, or when specifically invited to do so. There are many reasons that people might do this. Here I will examine just two: (a) a habit of integrating beliefs stored under different names—either quite generally, or with respect to particular names; and (b) having good reason to integrate beliefs.

6.6.1 Habit

One way that a person might get in the habit of integrating beliefs might simply be an individual tendency: if what I find so fascinating about the Superman stories is the fact that every clumsy, embarrassing action of wimpy Clark's is also an action of Superman's (and vice versa), I'll reflect on the identity a lot, and I will make many of inferences (e.g. *that's* Superman *spilling the coffee, stuttering, and hesitating to make eye contact! That's clumsy, pathetic* Clark *swooping down to save the Nobel laureates from the oncoming trolley car!*). The fact that I do this when reading the comic books means that I will be more likely to do this when presented with sentences like (1) and (1*). I might have such habits with respect to particular double lives, or—just as plausibly—with respect to double lives in general.

Another way that I might get in the habit of integrating beliefs is a professional one. If I spend a lot of time thinking about substitution inferences in certain ways, I may well develop strong inclinations to integrate beliefs. Suppose I teach philosophy of language. Then one of the things I probably teach every year is that substitution of co-referential names succeeds in the absence of opacity-producing operators. I give my students many examples to show this. I read papers from my students with their own examples. The result is that I get a great deal of practice at making substitution inferences in such sentences. This doesn't mean that I will always store my beliefs in an integrated way—I still need to follow comic book plots, after all. But when confronted with sentences like (1) and (2), I know just what is supposed to follow—I have a lot of practice producing it, and I may do so very easily.

I don't know how common such professional habits may be. Anecdotal observations suggest to me that anti-substitution intuitions about simple sentences *are* weaker among philosophers of language than among other philosophers. (It would be interesting to study this more fully.) However, there are obviously many philosophers of language for whom this isn't the case (e.g. Forbes, Moore, Pitt and Predelli). The explanation put forward in this chapter does not predict that philosophers of language will always form these habits, or that these habits will always affect their intuitions. Instead, it merely makes room for this possibility.

6.6.2 Good reason

The explanation offered here predicts that in cases where people have good reason not to integrate their beliefs (as with double lives), they will be less likely to do so than in cases where they lack such good reason (as with 'James Bartlett'/'the lawyer'). Another reasonable prediction would be that when subjects have good reason *to* integrate, they will be more willing to do so. Of course, it seems unlikely that subjects will *always* have good reason (on balance) to integrate—if we're to keep track of double lives, we need to keep our beliefs separate to at least some extent. But some of us might well have good reason to integrate beliefs after reflecting in the right sort of way.

What could count as such a good reason? Well, one obvious sort of reason would be a belief in a particular semantic theory. If I am a Fregean and, after much thought and careful study, I take Fregeanism to be well-supported, then I have good reason to believe that substitution of co-referential names always succeeds in contexts which lack opacity-producing operators, and that it may fail in contexts where such operators are present. If, again after much study and thought, I decide that Naïve Millianism is right, I will have good reason to believe that substitution of co-referential names always succeeds—in any context. In either case, I have good reason to integrate my *Superman* and *Clark* beliefs. I won't do so all the time—I want to be follow comic book plots efficiently, after all. But when I reflect on substitution inferences, things will be different. Suppose I'm presented with (1) and (1*). Like many people, I will probably have some initial inclination to think that they differ in truth value—this inclination arises from the way that I segregate my beliefs in order to follow comic book plots. But I quickly notice that the sentences involve co-referential names, and that they lack opacity-producing operators. I remember that I have a well-founded belief that substitution must succeed in such contexts. This belief is a strong and well-supported one. The strength of this belief will help me to overcome any residual resistance to integrating my beliefs: I *know* it's the right thing to do, so I do it. These theorists will have no difficulty casting aside their anti-substitution intuitions. The intuitions will seem (and perhaps be) weaker than those of others, since they will be easily and quickly overcome when beliefs are integrated.

Not every Millian or Fregean will, of course, do what is suggested above. Some Fregeans will not find their initial intuitions overcome by their well-supported conviction that substitution must be acceptable in simple sentences. These Fregeans may do any of a number of things: they may (like Forbes) decide that Frege was wrong to take substitution to fail only in special contexts—and attempt to find an account with these results. They may also decide that their intuitions, persistent as they are, are wrong. Such Fregeans (like Alex Barber) will look for an explanation of these mistakes. Some Millians will find themselves with lingering anti-substitution intuitions about simple sentences despite their well-supported conviction that such intuitions are wrong. For the Millian, this will probably be a familiar position: after all, they almost certainly have lingering anti-substitution intuitions about belief reports despite their conviction that such intuitions must be wrong. Theorists like these Millians and Fregeans find the habit of segregating beliefs to be too strong to be easily overcome by even well-supported convictions that such segregation is a mistake in certain instances. They will have intuitions that need explaining away, if they are to maintain their views. And this also makes perfect sense on the explanation put forward in this chapter.

6.7 WHY WE TALK THE WAY WE DO

The account sketched above focuses exclusively on explaining intuitions. But, as Graeme Forbes (forthcoming) has rightly pointed out, this is not all that needs explaining. We also need to explain why it is that speakers utter sentences like (6), below. (They do in fact utter such sentences: as noted in chapter 1, it has appeared in print.)

(6) Shostakovich always signalled his connections to the classical traditions of St Petersburg, even if he was forced to live in Leningrad.[11]

Facts about how we understand an utterance of a sentence like this can explain our intuitions about it, but they cannot explain why speakers utter this sentence. As Forbes rightly notes, the speakers making utterances like this are perfectly aware of the identities in question, so such lack of awareness cannot explain their utterances either—particularly

[11] *NY Review of Books* (2004). 10 June, p. 14.

since, he claims, they take themselves to be 'communicating the plain truth' (Forbes 2006: 167). (Forbes takes this formulation to be neutral between saying the truth and otherwise communicating it.)

Fortunately, the explanation offered in this chapter can readily be extended to cover such cases. We will begin by asking what is puzzling about utterances like (6).

A speaker who utters (6) seemingly presupposes a contrast between living in St Petersburg and living in Leningrad.

(6) Shostakovich always signalled his connections to the classical traditions of St Petersburg, even if he was forced to live in Leningrad.[12]

But if St Petersburg is Leningrad, there can be no such contrast. This is why an utterance of (6*) is unquestionably odd.

(6*) Shostakovich always signalled his connections to the classical traditions of Leningrad, even if he was forced to live in Leningrad.

(Whether this presupposition is semantically relevant is controversial, and so it is not obvious that (6*) is false. However, it is uncontroversially very odd.) No sane, sincere speaker who is aware that 'St Petersburg' and 'Leningrad' co-refer would utter (6*), and yet they do utter (6). And, when they do so, they take themselves to communicate a truth. How can this be?

The answer is simple. Sometimes, as argued earlier in this chapter, enlightened speakers well aware of particular identities will fail to make all the inferences that they could from the relevant identity claims. Sometimes, as we are all well aware, speakers use falsehoods in an effort to convey truths. These facts are perfectly sufficient to explain the example above.

The utterer of (6) knows that St Petersburg is Leningrad, and indeed reflects on this at the time that he utters (6). Nonetheless, he may think that (6) is true, and not odd. This is because he simply doesn't use his knowledge of the identity in question to infer from (6) to (6*), which might give him pause. (We have already discussed at length how this is possible.) He thinks that (6) is true, and so he utters it. Alternatively, an utterer of (6) may well make the relevant inference and realise that the sentence, taken literally, is false or at least very odd, yet use it trying to convey a non-odd truth. He may view this utterance as a case of the

---

[12] *NY Review of Books* (2004). 10 June, p. 14.

poetic license that allows one to convey significant truths by uttering literally false sentences. There is nothing unusual about a speaker using a falsehood in order to convey a truth. Moreover, this second scenario need not be cashed out in terms of the intuition-matching implicatures that have proved so problematic. All we need is some proposition that the speaker intends to convey by his utterance. This need not be grasped by the audience, and it need not have truth conditions that match our intuitions. The speaker's utterance could be adequately explained by her desire to convey any of a number of different propositions. For example:

(6C) Shostakovich didn't much care for the Communist regime.
(6C') Shostakovich's music evolved out of old Russian traditions.
(6C") Shostakovich's music didn't fit well with the Soviet style.

In short: although this chapter (and indeed this book) have focused on explaining our intuitions about simple sentence puzzle cases, the explanation offered can be easily extended to also explain our utterances.

6.8 HOW OFTEN WILL THIS HAPPEN?

There are many co-referential names in the world other than the ones that figure prominently in the substitution literature. For example, I alone have several names: 'Jenny', 'Jenny Saul', 'Jennifer Saul', 'Jennifer M. Saul', 'Jennifer Mather Saul', 'J.M. Saul'. There are also names that others use for me that I don't myself use: 'Jennifer Drainville-Saul', 'Jennifer Drainville', etc. (I think, despite my non-endorsement, these are probably still names for me in the dialects of the phone company, the gas company, the benighted relatives, etc.) One might worry that the story sketched here would wrongly predict simple sentence anti-substitution intuitions associated with all of these names.

I think this worry is misplaced. The story sketched here does indeed make room for simple sentence anti-substitution intuitions about all of these names, but (a) I think this is the right thing to do; and (b) this is very different from predicting that such intuitions will actually occur in every case.

What this chapter's explanation would predict is the following: if people learn information about me under two different names that they know to be co-referential, they are indeed likely to initially set up separate nodes for the information learned under the two names. We know they tend do this, after all, with information learned under a name or a description. They are only *likely* to do this because they may well not—seeing a drawing of the individual in question eliminated the tendency to do this with names and descriptions, and seeing some image of me or seeing me in person might well do the same for the name-name case. If they do not set up separate nodes for the two names, they will definitely not have simple sentence anti-substitution intuitions involving them. Even if people set up separate nodes, they may quickly become aware that there is no good reason to keep information associated with the different names separate. As a result, they may very quickly and efficiently integrate information, again failing to have anti-substitution intuitions.

However, the explanation here does make room for the possibility that people may take there to be good reason to keep information separate, and that as a result they may have simple sentence anti-substitution intuitions. For example, suppose that under 'J. Saul' I publish papers in philosophy of language endorsing Grice's theory of implicature, but under 'Jennifer Mather Saul' I publish papers in feminism arguing that this theory presupposes a phallocentric individualism that serves to support the patriarchy. It might then be very useful for one who cared about my views in both areas (though I can't really imagine who this would be, especially if I held these views!) to segregate information learned under the two names (even if they knew them to co-refer). Anti-substitution simple sentence intuitions might well arise under these circumstances. Depending on one's perspective, for example, either of the following might seem true:

(7) J. Saul is a reliable source of information, but Jennifer Mather Saul has crazy views and shouldn't be trusted.
(7*) Jennifer Mather Saul is a feminist, but J. Saul is a tool of the patriarchy.

I take it to be virtue of the theory sketched here that it would allow for this possibility.

6.9 SUMMARY

We have seen that a wide variety of theorists hold that we have different mental representations when we encounter (1) and (1*)—no matter what semantic content these sentences are assigned. We have also seen that psychological experiments suggest a tendency to segregate information known to be about a single individual, when that information is learned under more than one label for the individual. I have suggested that such segregation will be more likely, and harder to break down, when there is good reason to segregate information—and that in double life cases there is very good reason for segregating. Finally, I have shown how such segregation may give rise to anti-substitution intuitions about simple sentences (and noted some factors that could cause variation in willingness to integrate). This explanation is entirely independent of commitments to Millianism or Fregeanism. The intuitions would plausibly arise via these processes no matter what the content of simple sentences is—whether (1) and (1*) express different propositions, as the Fregean would have it, or the same proposition, as the Millian would have it. Moreover, this explanation does not depend in any way on (1) and (1*) *actually* having different truth values. Indeed, it assumes that they do not. We have already seen the failure of many attempts to provide accounts that yield different truth values for (1) and (1*)—prospects for this approach do not look good. Now we have seen that all of the observed intuitions can be explained much more simply, by pointing to and building on some widely accepted and some independently plausible claims about cognitive architecture and processing. Given that we *can* explain the intuitions this way, with minimal theoretical commitments, and given the difficulty of explaining them in other ways, it seems to me reasonable for theorists of many sorts to endorse the sort of explanation of intuitions offered here.

6.10 BEYOND THE SPECULATIVE?

The account suggested above is highly speculative and under-supported by current empirical evidence. This is not, it seems to me, surprising. The account sketched, after all, is meant to be a story of how psychological processing affects our truth-conditional intuitions about simple sentences involving co-referential names. This is clearly an empirical matter. Yet, as far as I have been able to ascertain, only two experiments have ever been done on how we process sentences with co-referential terms—and these experiments involved name/description pairs. The available evidence base, then, is pretty slim.

We need not, however, remain forever in the realm of the speculative. An account of our intuitions that is based on psychological processing considerations can and should be either supported or undermined by empirical data. This section suggests some ways that such supporting or undermining data might be discovered. In so doing, it responds to a further worry: that psychological accounts like the one I have suggested are far too easy to come by. Such accounts may well be easy to suggest, but they are also, it seems to me, quite insecure: not only can philosophical arguments be made against them, but empirical data might well show them to be utterly misguided.

6.10.1 Testing co-referential names

Anderson's experiments all involved co-referential name-description pairs. He found that subjects were slow to integrate information learned under one term with information learned under the other—unless they were taught the identities with the aid of drawings. I have suggested that this shows a tendency to keep information learned under different labels separate unless given good reason to integrate. However, many alternative hypotheses are possible. One is that Anderson's findings resulted from the fact that he used name-description pairs, rather than co-referential names. Subjects might, for example, be especially reluctant to integrate information from different nodes if one of these nodes bears a label that is richer in information content than the other—as a description generally is, when compared with a name. If this is right—or if name-description pairs are essential to Anderson's findings for some other reason—then performing similar experiments with co-referential names should give very different results.

Let's consider in slightly more detail what we might learn from testing co-referential name pairs.

- *Outcome 1:* Subjects are just as slow to integrate information learned under different co-referential names as they were to integrate information in Anderson's experiments involving name-description pairs. This result would fit well with this chapter's suggested explanation.

- *Outcome 2:* Subjects are even slower to integrate information learned under different co-referential names than they were to integrate information in Anderson's experiments involving name-description pairs. This would fit very well with the explanation suggested in this chapter. (Although it would raise the interesting question of why should subjects be slower with co-referential names.)

- *Outcome 3:* Subjects are faster to integrate information learned under different co-referential names than they were at integrating information in Anderson's experiments. However, they still exhibit a significant time-lag. This result might well pose problems for the explanation suggested in this chapter. However, I don't think that it does.

1. The possible problem: Although the explanation given above does not actually involve the claim that reluctance to integrate will be the same with name pairs as it is with name/description pairs, it needs to be able to explain the recalcitrant intuitions that some subjects display. This might seem difficult if such integration is quicker and easier than with name/description pairs.

2. The response: It could be that the larger time-lag in Anderson's experiments is due to his use of incomplete descriptions. Since there are many individuals who fit the description 'the lawyer', subjects may need more processing time to work out which individual is under discussion. (This could be tested by comparing incomplete and complete descriptions.) More importantly, however, all that is needed for the explanation given above is a significant time lag, suggesting that separate nodes have been set up. The explanation of recalcitrant intuitions invoked factors such as confidence in truth-conditional intuitions, lack of confidence in particular inferences and knowledge of the deceptiveness of surface structure. None of these suggestions has been undermined.

• *Outcome 4:* Subjects are extremely fast at integrating information learned under different co-referential names. This result would pose serious problems for the explanation sketched in this chapter: it suggests that Anderson's results may have arisen from some special feature of name-description pairs. If this is right, then claims about co-referential name pairs based on these results are deeply misguided.

Of course, reluctance to integrate information may be affected by not just what terms are used, but also by the stories that are told about the characters involved. I discuss this possibility in the next section.

6.10.2 Reason to separate information

I have suggested that when subjects have good reason to keep information associated with different labels separate, they will be more likely to set up and maintain separate nodes for the different labels. This thought plays an important role in my explanation of anti-substitution simple sentence intuitions, and in particular to my explanation of their resilience. Yet it is purely speculative, wholly unsupported by empirical data. It is, however, highly testable. One way to test it would be to look again at name-description pairs, as Anderson does, but to weave these name-descriptions pairs into tales of double lives. For example, the Identity Learning phase of the experiments would involve telling subjects James Bartlett is the lawyer, but that he is embarrassed to tell his anti-establishment friends that he has become a lawyer, instead maintaining the cover story that he makes a living by selling the occasional painting. One could even use different drawings of James—clean-cut, in a suit, for 'the lawyer', scruffy, in a paint spattered smock, for 'James Bartlett'. The Other Learning phase could remain the same, as could the Verification phase.

Some possible outcomes:

- *Outcome 1:* Subjects are slower to answer questions that require integrating information from the different nodes than they were in Anderson's experiments. This would show that having good reason to separate information associated with different labels, as in cases of double lives, does indeed cause a reluctance to integrate such information. This would provide some support for my claims.

- *Outcome 2:* Subjects are no slower at answering questions that require integrating information from the different nodes than they were in Anderson's experiments. This might show that my suggestion was wrong: having good reason to keep information separate does not actually slow the integration process. However, it might show instead that I had failed to give subjects adequate reason not to integrate. After all, the simple sentences that provoke intuitions of substitution failure are generally ones in which subjects have quite a rich body of information to draw on about the double lives in question—or at least substantial familiarity with the two labels. It might be that quite a lot of information is required to provoke an increased resistance to integration. (Recall that there *is* resistance to integration even without good reason for such resistance.) This possibility could be tested by offering subjects much richer information about the double lives, or by drawing upon familiar examples.

These experiments, however, only test name-description pairs. It would be important to also test pairs of co-referential names, with and without stories (rich or brief), of double lives, and drawings of the same person assuming different looks—otherwise one might worry that any delay in integration was due in part to some special feature of name-description pairs. It is also possible that the very existence of different co-referential names suggests that there is good reason not to integrate—so this effect might be stronger with co-referential name pairs.

It might well turn out that having good reason not to integrate information learned under different labels has no effect whatsoever on tendencies to keep such information segregated. If this was shown, then an important part of my explanation of simple sentence intuitions would have to be abandoned.

6.10.3 Simple sentence intuitions

I have claimed that there are many cases involving simple sentences in which, intuitively, substitution of co-referential names fails. Anecdotally, this seems to be true. Philosophers often rest content with such reflections, but it seems to me worth investigating empirically the existence and resilience of such intuitions. One reason for this is that some philosophers, as noted earlier, do not seem to have these intuitions. More importantly, though, it seems to me a mistake to rely on my own reflections and those of other philosophers, when I am making empirical claims about how humans process sentences containing co-referential names.

It is important, then, not just to conduct experiments that mirror Anderson's, but also ones that test responses to collections of sentences like those that have been the main topic of this book. We need to know what happens, for instance, when we tell people that (1) is true and ask them whether (1*) must also be true.

(1) Clark Kent went into the phone booth and Superman came out.
(1*) Superman went into the phone booth and Clark Kent came out.

Although it is probably safe to assume that everyone to be tested will know that (2) is true, we need to know the effect of reminding subjects that it is.

(2) Superman is Clark Kent.

So we should also test to see what subjects say when we tell them that (1) and (2) are true and ask them whether (1*) must be true.

Conducting these experiments will give us some valuable information.

- *Outcome 1:* Subjects insist that (1*) must be true in both versions of the experiment. The most obvious interpretation of this result is that the whole premise of this book is undermined: people don't, after all, have anti-substitution intuitions about simple sentences. However, it is important to remember that the sentences would have been presented without much context—it may be that a fuller set-up would produce different results. It may also be that subjects are poor at the task of holding fixed certain facts while considering what else must be true. Nonetheless, it has to be admitted that this result would undermine much of this book. This risk is one that comes with caring about empirical data.

- *Outcome 2:* Subjects deny that (1*) must be true in the first version of the experiment, but insist that it must be in the second version. If this happens, it seems that anti-substitution intuitions about simple sentences are not resilient. Although they are initially present, they are easily undermined. If this is right, then only part of the explanation suggested in this chapter is needed: we only need to explain initial anti-substitution intuitions. (But what should we say, then, about philosophers who seem to have such strong and resilient anti-substitution intuitions that they construct whole theories to accommodate them? They are, apparently, special cases, and can be dealt with as such. Perhaps their intuitions are too theory-laden to be taken seriously, or perhaps they are simply very idiosyncratic cases.)

- *Outcome 3:* Subjects deny that (1*) must be true, in both versions of the experiment. This result accords with the assumptions on which much of this book is based: that there are resilient anti-substitution intuitions about simple sentences, which persist even once subjects have been reminded of the relevant identity sentences.

A further sort of experiment would also be valuable. In my discussion of the Enlightenment Problem, I have made various claims about how intuitions do or do not change as we learn about whether the speaker and/or audience are enlightened. These are empirical claims, and testable ones. They should, then, be tested. If they turn out to be false, then one sort of objection to other accounts fails (though the Aspect Problem may well remain). This would not show the account proposed in this chapter to be wrong, but it would weaken the case against alternative accounts. Finally, it is worth testing whether intuitions are the same about cases involving name change (like 'Leningrad'/'St Petersburg') and cases involving 'double lives'. If intuitions differ, it may be that different explanations are appropriate for the different sorts of cases.[13]

6.10.4 How much can be shown?

Suppose the research suggested above is done. How much will that show us? Well, as noted above, certain results would count against the account outlined here. Empirical research, then, could show this account to be untenable. But what if the results are favourable to it? Would this show it to be correct? Unfortunately (for me), it would not. If the experiments suggested above are done, and the outcomes are favourable to the account, that would provide some support—in that disconfirmation was possible, but it did not occur. However, all that would be shown is that empirical data are consistent with it. Other possible accounts would by no means be ruled out by such empirical data. Such results, for example, are perfectly consistent with other accounts of simple sentence intuitions. After all, those accounts make no commitments whatsoever regarding mental processing. (It seems to me, though, that those accounts can be ruled out on the philosophical grounds outlined earlier.)

The most that could be said for my account, in the best of circumstances, would be something like this: Other accounts of simple sentence intuitions do not succeed. This account, which requires the truth of certain empirical claims about psychology, can explain our intuitions. The empirical claims in question have been tested and not disconfirmed, and they seem plausible. This account deserves to be taken seriously, and in the absence of promising alternatives it should be provisionally accepted.

Of course, we are not yet in the best of circumstances—we need a great deal more empirical data before we will be. But I hope that I have shown the approach outlined above to be plausible and at least somewhat appealing, and also to have shown how further relevant empirical research might proceed. My claims, then, are really quite modest. But it seems to me that the sort of approach suggested here is a novel and interesting one, well worth considering further—and perhaps applying to other problems.

---

[13] This is what Zimmerman (2005) suggests.

Appendix A: Extending the Account

As Stefano Predelli (2001) has emphasised,[1] terms other than names may also give rise to intuitions that feel to be somehow *of the same sort* as those that have been the topic of this book. In some of these cases, what is going on is clearly not anything to do with substitution of co-referential terms, and yet a feeling remains that a solution to the problems that have been our main focus should also be extendable to these cases. Predelli writes, 'the reactions elicited by [non-name cases] are so importantly similar to the Intuition regarding [name cases] that any satisfactory analysis of the latter must be applicable to the former' (p. 312). I am far from certain that the condition Predelli imposes must be right: cases may feel similar and yet turn out to be quite different. However, I think it is a virtue of the solution proposed here that it can quite readily be extended to non-name cases.

A.1 EXAMPLES

We will begin by looking at some of these non-name cases.

A.1.1 Descriptions

Assume that Superman is the worst-dressed superhero and Clark Kent the shyest reporter. Despite this assumption, (1) might seem true and (1*) false, even if you also know that (2) is true.

(1) The shyest reporter went into the phone booth and the worst-dressed superhero came out.
(1*) The worst-dressed superhero went into the phone booth and the shyest reporter came out.
(2) Superman is Clark Kent.

This case is straightforwardly a problem regarding apparent substitution failure. Despite the fact that the descriptions 'the worst-dressed superhero' and 'the shyest reporter' co-refer, it seems, intuitively, that substitution of one for the other in a simple sentence may result in a change of truth value.

---

[1] I also discuss some cases of this sort in Saul (1997), at 104 and footnote 13, 108.

A.1.2 Indexicals

Imagine that the first occurrence of 'he' is accompanied by pointing at the be-caped hero in the Superhero Book of Mug Shots, and the second occurrence by pointing at the shy reporter lurking in the corner of the room. (We will set aside interesting but irrelevant issues regarding deferred ostension.)

(3) He hit Lex Luther more times than he did.

This utterance seems like it might well be true, even if we know that the same individual is being indicated by both pointings. This is not strictly speaking a *substitution* problem, but it seems rather closely parallel to the problem posed by the familiar (4):

(4) Superman leaps more tall buildings than Clark Kent does.

In both cases, we have a comparison between an individual A and himself, in which A is said to F more often than A does. And yet the claim seems intuitively true.

A.1.3 Quantifiers

Clark Kent is sitting in the conference room with his shy colleagues, Art and Bart, all of them bemoaning their lack of dates for the upcoming Reporters' Ball.[2] (5) seems likely to be true of this situation:

(5) Nobody in the conference room is successful with women.

But if Clark Kent is in the conference room, then Superman is also in the conference room. Since Superman is a noted heart-throb, (5) should not seem true. This example is especially interesting, since it does not seem to involve substitution failure. Nor is it obviously analogous to examples involving substitution failure, like (3) is. However, Predelli is right to note that it *feels* like an example of a phenomenon very similar to those that have been our focus; and also right to claim that an account of the latter would ideally explain this sort of case.

As Predelli notes, it is not entirely obvious how accounts like Barber's, Forbes's, or Moore's would cope with these cases. A psychological processing-based account, however, does not face the same problems. There are several sorts of stories about psychological processes that could explain these intuitions. I will not be claiming that the specific stories suggested here are correct. My goal is simply to show that the sort of solution I have proposed for other cases can be extended to cover the cases in this appendix. In all these cases, the exact details can only be discovered by empirical research. I will be relatively brief

---

[2] This example based on Predelli (2001: 311).

with my sketches here, assuming that Chapter 6 will allow the reader to fill them out more fully if they wish to do so (and also that they might rather be boiled in oil than hear further details at this point).

A.2 THE ACCOUNT

A.2.1 Descriptions

We'll start with (1) and (1*):

(1) The shyest reporter went into the phone booth and the worst-dressed superhero came out.
(1*) The worst-dressed superhero went into the phone booth and the shyest reporter came out.

Our problem (as laid out above) is to explain why it is that even if I know (1), (2) and (6) to be true, I might still think that (1*) is false.

(2) Superman is Clark Kent.
(6) Superman is the worst-dressed superhero and Clark Kent is the shyest reporter.

How might this happen? Quite easily. In order to realise that (1)'s truth guarantees that of (1*) from the information given above, I need to make some inferences. I need to use (6) to get me from (1) to (7):

(7) Clark Kent went into the phone booth and Superman came out.

Then I need to use (2) to get me from (7) to (7*):

(7*) Superman went into the phone booth and Clark Kent came out.

Finally, I need to use (6) again to get me to (1*):

(1*) The worst-dressed superhero went into the phone booth and the shyest reporter came out.

All this is far from simple to do, and I might easily fail to do it.[3]

Alternatively, I might process the information (1) gives me by storing it under the names 'Superman' and 'Clark Kent'. I don't normally think in terms of 'the shyest reporter' or 'the worst-dressed superhero', so when I encounter these phrases I ask myself who they refer to. I realise that (1) is telling me the same thing that (7) would tell me.

---

[3] As I described the example initially, all these inferences would be needed. An alternative example might work from the assumption that the shyest reporter is the worst-dressed superhero. Fewer inferences would be needed in this case to get from (1) to (1*), but I might still fail to make the requisite inference, for all the reasons discussed in Chapter 6.

(7) Clark Kent went into the phone booth and Superman came out.

Now I encounter (1*), and carry out a similar inference, realising it tells me what (7*) would tell me:

(7*) Superman went into the phone booth and Clark Kent came out.

If this is how I think about (1) and (1*)—as seems perfectly plausible—then the explanation offered in Chapter 6 can simply be transferred over, from this point on.

A.2.2 Indexicals

Our puzzle case here is (3).

(3) He hit Lex Luther more times than he did.

One who witnesses an utterance of (3) accompanied by pointings at appropriate photos will access their *Superman* node when considering the first half of the comparison, and their *Clark* node when considering the second half. *Fights villains* is a rather prominent bit of information stored under *Superman,* and *is wimpy* is a similarly prominent bit of information stored under *Clark.* Consulting this stored information, one will take (3) to be perfectly plausible. Of course, reflecting on (2) could lead one to change one's mind about this.

(2) Superman is Clark Kent.

But, for all the reasons discussed in Chapter 6, this might or might not occur.

A.2.3 Quantifiers

Here our concern is with sentence (5), uttered when Clark and his shy reporter friends are sitting in the conference room:

(5) Nobody in the conference room is successful with women.

(5) seems like a true description of this state of affairs, even if one knows that (2) is true.

(2) Superman is Clark Kent.

This is fairly readily explained. When considering the truth of (5), given the set-up for the example we access our *Clark* node, and not our *Superman* node. Given the information at that node, and the other information presented with the example, (5) will seem true to us. We are not in the habit of automatically accessing information from the *Superman* node. If we did access this information, we would see that (5) is false. But we do not do that, so we don't. Even when presented with (2), we may still fail to infer that

(8) is true—for all the same sorts of reasons that we have discussed in Chapter 6.

(8) Superman is in the conference room.

If we don't make this inference or a similar one, we will have no reason to doubt the truth of (5).

Appendix B: Belief Reporting

When simple sentence puzzle cases were introduced, they seemed to have a bearing on more traditional substitution puzzle cases, like those involving belief reports. Our question in this appendix is whether this still seems to be true. I will argue that it is, and that what we have learned from studying simple sentences has the potential to offer us new approaches to these belief-reporting puzzle cases as well.

B.1 A CHALLENGE TO ANTI-NAÏVE MILLIANS

In Chapter 1, I argued that simple sentences pose a special challenge to those who oppose Naïve Millianism.[1] Let's revisit this argument now, to see if it still seems right. The problem simple sentences posed for opponents came in the form of a dilemma. Such theorists insist that substitution must be blocked in belief-reporting sentences, and they offer theories designed to do this. Once simple sentence puzzle cases are appreciated, these theorists are faced with a choice:

- *Option 1:* Extend their theory so that it blocks substitution in simple sentences as well as in sentences containing standard substitution-blocking constructions.
- *Option 2:* Maintain that our anti-substitution intuitions about simple sentences are in error. On this option, the opponent of Naïve Millianism must explain away anti-substitution intuitions about simple sentences while insisting that it is unacceptable for the Naïve Millian to explain away anti-substitution intuitions about belief reports. She will, then, need to offer a very good reason to suppose that anti-substitution intuitions about belief reports demand a kind of respect that those about simple sentences do not.

This problem remains, and indeed our explorations have shown it to be more pressing still. We have canvassed several efforts to block substitution in simple sentences—either by extending existing theories (Forbes) or by formulating new ones (Moore, Pitt, Predelli). All of these failed. Option 1 now looks substantially less promising than it looked in Chapter 1. The most promising response to anti-substitution simple sentence intuitions seems to be to claim

---

[1] They also pose a challenge for Millians, but that challenge can be met, it seems to me, by the theory sketched in Chapter 6.

that they are in error. I have suggested that a psychologically-based explanation of these errors holds considerable potential for success. The anti-Naïve Millian who accepts all this will opt for Option 2. But if they do this they must accept the additional burden mentioned in Option 2. *Despite* their willingness to explain away anti-substitution intuitions about simple sentences, they must continue to insist that such explanations are unacceptable in the case of belief-reporting intuitions. The challenge of justifying such differential treatment remains.

B.2 A FURTHER CHALLENGE TO ANTI-NAÏVE MILLIANS

The challenge outlined above is heightened if anti-substitution intuitions about belief reports and simple sentences can be explained in the same way. To see this, consider an opponent of Naïve Millianism who has been convinced by the arguments of this book so far. Such a person accepts that the best way to explain simple sentence intuitions is via the psychological, processing-based explanation offered in Chapter 6. Now suppose that an explanation of the same sort can be offered for anti-substitution intuitions about belief reports. One who has already accepted an explanation of just this sort for simple sentence intuitions must now explain why this sort of explanation of intuitions is acceptable for simple sentences but not for belief reports. In particular, if anti-substitution intuitions about belief-reporting can be explained by drawing only upon resources that the theorist is *already committed to,* they owe us a reason for rejecting such an explanation.

With this in mind, our next project is to explore whether such a psychological explanation of belief-reporting intuitions is available. I will argue that it is.

B.2.1 Can the Naïve Millian explain away belief-reporting intuitions in the same way as simple sentence intuitions?

Before attempting to answer this question, it will be worthwhile to review the situation of the Naïve Millian who attempts to explain away anti-substitution belief-reporting intuitions. According to the Naïve Millian, (1) and (1*) below express the same proposition and must have the same truth conditions.[2]

(1) Lois believes that Superman can fly.
(1*) Lois believes that Clark can fly.

---

[2] Reminder: I use the phrase 'truth conditions' to refer to the truth values of a sentence in a context, evaluated both at the actual world and at other possible worlds. Truth-conditional intuitions are intuitions about these truth values.

The problem the Naïve Millian faces is that of explaining why it is that we think, incorrectly, that (1) and (1*) may differ in truth value even though we know that (2) is true. (As noted in Chapter 1, it is only the intuitions of the enlightened—those who know that (2) is true—that are problematic to explain.)

(2) Superman is Clark.

The traditional approach has been to invoke matching propositions of some sort—most commonly, implicated ones. The approach to simple sentences suggested in Chapter 6 is to abandon this reliance on matching propositions. Instead, the thought is, we may be able to explain how our intuitions go astray by focusing on considerations of psychological processing. In some sense, any explanation of anti-substitution intuitions that relies upon cognitive processing rather than on matching propositions implicated, asserted, etc. is a relative of this explanation. However, the closer the relative the more interesting it will be. With that in mind, it is worth reminding ourselves of some of the key features of Chapter 6's explanation of simple sentence intuitions.

The explanation in Chapter 6:

(1) Makes use of the claim that we entertain different representations when we encounter sentences differing from each other only in the substitution of one co-referential name for another.
(2) Suggests that there are features of our cognitive architecture (in particular, a tendency to segregate information) that render us unlikely to make substitution inferences (even if these inferences are valid).
(3) Does not appeal to the entertainment of propositions whose truth values match those indicated by our intuitions.
(4) Suggests a variety of further factors that may play a role in producing resilient anti-substitution intuitions. These include:

   a. Failure to consider relevant identity;
   b. Lack of logical acumen;
   c. Lack of confidence in reasoning abilities;
   d. Strength of anti-substitution intuitions;
   e. Good reason to reject substitution;
   f. Knowledge that surface structure can be misleading;
   g. Habits of resistance to certain kinds of inference.

It seems to me that these resources can be used to offer an explanation of enlightened anti-substitution intuitions about belief-reporting sentences. We start by observing, along with nearly all other Naïve Millians, that sentences (1) and (1*) present the same proposition in different ways.

(1) Lois believes that Superman can fly.
(1*) Lois believes that Clark can fly.

When we consider these sentences and entertain the proposition that they express, we represent it to ourselves in different ways. As result, it is not immediately apparent to us that (1) and (1*) must take the same truth value. Even though (1*) follows from (1) and (2), and we know that (2) is true, we may easily not make this inference.

(2) Superman is Clark.

After all, as we noted in the last chapter, we don't always make all of the inferences that we can. We may have simply failed to reflect upon (2)'s truth.

Our cognitive architecture may make it unlikely that we will reflect upon (2) when we read (1) and (1*). Suppose it is right that we store information about individuals at separate nodes associated with those individuals (or, as we saw in the last chapter, with particular labels/representations for those individuals). Then, when we read and accept (1), we will store the information it gives us at our *Lois* node—perhaps in the form of sentence (1) or its mental correlate. When we read and accept (2), we won't store the information it gives us at our *Lois* node—we'll store it at our *Superman* and *Clark* nodes, perhaps in the form of (2) or its mental correlate. When we reflect upon (1) and (1*)'s truth values, we do so by consulting the information at our *Lois* node—after all, the sentences are about her beliefs. Reflecting on (2) would require us to shift from the *Lois* node to another node, and make the inferences licensed by information at both nodes. It doesn't seem unreasonable at all that we might refrain from doing this.

But this explanation is insufficient. Even when we are reminded of (2)'s truth, invited to reflect upon it, and explicitly invited to consider the inference from (1) and (2) to (1*), we show little tendency to infer that (1)'s truth guarantees the truth of (1*)—or, more simply, to infer from (1) and (2) to (1*). Obviously, cognitive architecture alone cannot explain this—we have, after all, been given reason to reflect on (2). Why don't we make the inference?

One reason is that we may have very good reason to believe in (1)'s truth and (1*)'s falsehood. As David Braun (1998: 586–90) has argued, a person may have good evidence for believing that sentences like these take different truth values, and for believing that particular substitution inferences are invalid—even if they are valid. What sort of evidence could underpin this will vary. One way that we could come to believe that (1) is true and (1*) false could be by observing Lois's behaviour. Suppose, for example, that Lois says things like 'Superman can fly but Clark can't'. She might also ask Superman, be-caped, for a flying lift home while only asking Clark, be-suited, to share a cab. These observations would serve as evidence for the truth values we have assigned (1) and (1*), and it would be very difficult for any argument to undermine it—because we will simply have more confidence in our judgments of truth value than in the inference that would show these judgments to be wrong.

Often, though, we are presented with substitution puzzle cases for which we don't have this sort of observational evidence. We are presented, for example, with a sentence like (3), and asked to reflect on whether (3*) might differ in truth value, given that (4) is true.

(3) Ethel believes that Bob Dylan is a singer.
(3*) Ethel believes that Robert Zimmerman is a singer.
(4) Bob Dylan is Robert Zimmerman.

We can't draw on the same sort of evidence to make this decision—for one thing, we know almost nothing about Ethel. Instead, we need to draw on our knowledge of people and their beliefs. Perhaps we reflect on cases like this that we have known—in which we did have observational evidence. Perhaps we reflect, more generally, on our knowledge about the way that the world does or doesn't impact on what people believe. In any case, we may well have good evidence that it's possible for sentences like (3) and (3*) to be true, despite the truth of (4). In the face of such good evidence, we may quite reasonably reject the (in fact valid) inference from (3) and (4) to (3*).

As with simple sentences, the above may be equally true for the logically insecure and the logically savvy and confident. The insecure will doubt the argument from (1) and (2) to (1*) because they doubt their reasoning abilities. The savvy and confident will doubt it because they know how misleading surface structure can be.

A further factor may be the habits of inference-making and inference-resisting that we develop. Recall the suggestion above that information about Lois's beliefs will be stored at a *Lois* node, while information about Superman/Clark will not be. I suggested above that we will not automatically look outside the *Lois* node when reasoning about Lois's beliefs. Now I want to strengthen this thought: it seems to me very likely that we will have a well-established habit of looking only to information stored at our *A* node when reasoning about *A*'s beliefs. That is, we will be likely to seek out information about other beliefs that Lois has, information about what she has seen, or information about what she has heard. We will use this information to make inferences about what Lois believes. But we will be unlikely to look for information that is not information about Lois, and to use that information to make inferences about what Lois believes. These habits are ones that serve us well. Information that is not about A is generally not relevant to what A believes. Despite their prominence in the philosophical literature, substitution puzzle cases are not a regular feature of everyday life.[3] Well-established and useful habits may, then, cause us to resist substitution inferences that are in fact valid.

The story above seems to me to offer a good explanation of our anti-substitution intuitions about belief-reporting sentences. The question now is whether this explanation is of the same sort as that offered for our anti-substitution intuitions about simple sentences. This will, of course, depend

---

[3] Even in the case of substitution puzzle cases, such resistance may still be a good idea. It leads us, for example, to the false belief that (1*) isn't true; but it saves us from many other false beliefs—that Lois is about to ask the guy in the suit for a flying lift, that Lois thinks there is a guy who flies while wearing a suit, etc.

in part on how finely we individuate sorts of explanations—the explanations cannot of course be *exactly* the same, since they have (at least) a different subject matter. But it seems to me that a good case can be made for these explanations being, in some important sense, of the same sort. Here again are the key features of the simple sentence explanation, each followed by a discussion of similarities and differences between that explanation and the one suggested here:

(1) The simple sentence explanation makes use of the claim that we entertain different representations when we encounter sentences differing from each other only in the substitution of one co-referential name for another.
This feature appears, and plays an important role in the explanation.
(2) The simple sentence explanation suggests that there are features of our cognitive architecture (in particular, a tendency to segregate information) that render us unlikely to make substitution inferences (even if these inferences are valid).
Cognitive architecture plays an important role in the explanation above, as does the more specific claim that segregation of information can help to produce a reluctance to make substitution inferences. More specifically, it makes use of the fact that the belief expressed by (2) would not be stored at the same node as the belief expressed by (1).[4]
(3) The simple sentence explanation does not appeal to the entertainment of propositions whose truth values match those indicated by our intuitions.
Neither account makes any appeal to such intuition-matching propositions.
(4) Suggests a variety of further factors that may play a role in producing resilient anti-substitution intuitions. These include:

    a. Failure to consider relevant identity;
    b. Lack of logical acumen;
    c. Lack of confidence in reasoning abilities;
    d. Strength of anti-substitution intuitions;
    e. Good reason to reject substitution;
    f. Knowledge that surface structure can be misleading;
    g. Habits of resistance to certain kinds of inference.

Both accounts make use of these factors in explaining resilient anti-substitution intuitions.

It seems to me reasonable to claim that the account of belief-reporting intuitions suggested here is of the same sort as the account of simple sentence intuitions suggested in Chapter 6. If this is right, then one who accepts the account of simple sentence intuitions offered in the last chapter but rejects the account of belief-reporting intuitions sketched here owes us an explanation of this disparity. If this sort of account is adequate to explain away intuitions about simple sentences, why isn't it adequate to explain away intuitions about

---

[4] This is a different segregation claim from that employed in the simple sentence explanation. That explanation made use of the claim that we store information associated with different labels at different nodes (even when the labels are known to be co-referential). This claim plays no role in the explanation of belief-reporting intuitions.

belief reports? And if it is adequate to explain intuitions about belief reports, why *not* accept Naïve Millianism and an explanation like this of recalcitrant anti-substitution intuitions?

The challenge becomes more pressing still when we consider a key way that the explanations are similar: they draw on the same resources. One who has already accepted the explanation of simple sentence intuitions in Chapter 6 need not commit to any controversial new claims in order to explain away belief-reporting intuitions.

B.2.2 An objection and reply

The opponent of Naïve Millianism may reply that she has a perfectly principled reason for treating belief-reporting and simple sentence intuitions so differently. Anti-substitution intuitions about belief-reporting are, quite simply, stronger than anti-substitution intuitions about simple sentences. It is far easier, she may argue, to convince someone that (5) entails (5*) than that (6) entails (6*).

(5) Superman leaps more tall buildings than Clark Kent.
(5*) Superman leaps more tall buildings than Superman.
(6) Lois believes that Superman leaps more tall buildings than Clark Kent.
(6*) Lois believes that Superman leaps more tall buildings than Superman.

Because anti-substitution intuitions about belief-reporting are much stronger than those about simple sentences, they are deserving of more respect. It is acceptable, this line goes, to violate and explain away the relatively weak simple sentence intuitions; but it is not acceptable to do this with the stronger belief-reporting intuitions.

It is undeniable that at least some philosophers take there to be a significant difference in strength between the simple sentence intuitions I have drawn on here and belief-reporting intuitions. We should be careful, however, not to overstate this. Some philosophers clearly have extremely strong anti-substitution intuitions about simple sentences—the fact that most accounts of simple sentence intuitions in the literature uphold the anti-substitution intuitions is some indication of this. We should also bear in mind that most philosophers have accepted for a very long time that substitution only fails in certain special contexts, and that it is guaranteed to succeed in simple sentences. Many philosophers have aligned themselves in one way or another with theories that, in one way or another, incorporate or build on this presumption. Others have simply taken it for granted without caring a great deal about it. In either case, the idea that substitution could fail in simple sentences goes against long-standing convictions. In such circumstances, we should expect people to be resistant to it. The fact that any philosophers at all find themselves with strong anti-substitution intuitions about simple sentences is a significant one, as is the fact that many philosophers find themselves with at least *some* inclination against substituting. It is perhaps also significant that many philosophers of language will have had the experience of teaching students who are considerably less willing to substitute in simple sentences than they are supposed to be. This experience is some clue that the intuitions of ordinary people about these matters may be different from those of philosophers. Such conflicts, of course, are nothing new. And in many cases, there is good reason to prefer the intuitions of philosophers. But in this case, where the phenomenon in question (resistance to substitution in simple sentences) is one that goes against assumptions that have long been taken for granted by philosophers, there may be reason to prefer the intuitions of ordinary people.

Now put aside these concerns. Let's suppose that we have established that, for both philosophers and non-philosophers, anti-substitution intuitions about belief reports are generally significantly stronger than those about simple sentences. Would this difference in degree be sufficient to establish a difference in kind between belief reports and other sentences? I don't think it would be. After all, many phenomena have obvious, clear cases and less obvious, less clear cases. The obvious cases, most of us think, at least have the potential to help us to understand the less obvious ones. Take the distinction between lying and misleading, for example, and consider an utterance of (7), below.

(7) Amanda and Beau got married and had children.

If, as a matter of fact, Amanda and Beau had children before they got married, many people will—at least before they reflect carefully—consider this utterance to be a lie.

Those who take the speaker to have been merely misleading, rather than lying, will say that—although her utterance conveyed a falsehood (that the marriage preceded the children)—she did not say anything false. They can help to explicate this by pointing to other utterances in which people clearly mislead rather than lie. Suppose Alfred needs to buy petrol for his car and explains this to Bettina. Bettina replies 'there's a service station around the corner'. It turns out that the service station has been closed for the last 10 years and Bettina knows this, so she knew that Alfred could not buy petrol there. Did Bettina lie? Obviously not, but it is equally obvious that she misled Alfred, by conveying to him (without saying it) that he could buy petrol at the service station around the corner. Looking at this case makes it clear that sometimes we mislead rather than lie, by conveying rather than saying something false. Once this phenomenon has been brought to our attention, most of us will start to see the utterance of (7) as merely misleading rather than false. But not *all* of us will. And clearly our intuitions about (7) are less strong than our intuitions about the petrol station utterance. There is no doubt that the petrol station utterance is a clearer case of misleading by saying something true than (7) is. But this fact alone does not establish that the cases must be treated differently.

It is important to be clear on what I am arguing above: I am *not* suggesting that differences in strength of intuition are irrelevant to our theorising. That is clearly false. But what I am suggesting is that a difference in strength of intuition should not be taken as a decisive reason to treat cases differently. Indeed, we commonly treat cases alike even when intuitions differ in strength—and our acceptance of this practice is implicit in the fact that we frequently try to illuminate unclear cases by reflecting on clear ones.

A further point: even if we accept that anti-substitution belief-reporting intuitions are generally stronger than anti-substitution simple sentence intuitions, we must also acknowledge that there is considerable variation within each category—and even, perhaps, that some simple sentence anti-substitution intuitions are stronger than some belief-reporting anti-substitution intuitions. The fact that some anti-substitution intuitions regarding belief reports are weak is a familiar one. Indeed, we noted in Chapter 1 that not all belief-reporting utterances elicit any anti-substitution intuitions at all. Here we'll consider a new example. Suppose somebody I trust utters sentence (8):

(8) Caleb believes that Bush is an intelligent man.

I am shocked, and I want to pass this surprising information on to some of my fellow Democrats. So I utter (8*):

(8*) Caleb believes that W is an intelligent man.

My utterance, (8*), seems uncontroversially true. To know that (8*) is true we don't need to know whether or not Caleb has over heard 'W' as a nickname for Bush, or indeed anything else about how he thinks of Bush. Even if we learned that Caleb is unfamiliar with the name 'W', we would not change our minds.[5] We happily allow, then, that the substitution of 'W' for 'Bush' preserves truth value. We don't, then, have anti-substitution intuitions about this belief-reporting example. Compare this case to the familiar one of (9) and (9*), below.

(9) Clark Kent went into the phone booth, and Superman came out.
(9*) Superman went into the phone booth, and Clark Kent came out.

Suppose (9) is uttered as a description of the events witnessed on a Metropolis street. Assume that it is true. Intuitively, it does not seem to follow from this that (9*) must be true. Even if you are a philosopher whose anti-substitution intuitions regarding simple sentences are very weak—far weaker than most of your anti-substitution intuitions about belief reports—your anti-substitution intuition regarding (9) and (9*) is probably stronger than your anti-substitution intuition regarding (8) and (8*). Thus, there are some

---

[5] This is assuming that the context remains the same. If we switch, for example, to a case in which we're trying to predict what Caleb will write on his 'Intelligent Men of the 21st Century' quiz, our intuitions will shift as well.

anti-substitution intuitions about simple sentences that are stronger than some anti-substitution intuitions about belief reports. It is wrong, then, to insist that the contrast between belief-reporting and simple sentence anti-substitution intuitions is a clear and stark one, on which belief reports elicit strong anti-substitution intuitions and simple sentences elicit weak ones.

As a matter of fact, it seems to me that some comparative empirical study of anti-substitution intuitions would be immensely valuable. Philosophers of language generally assume that anti-substitution intuitions about belief-reporting sentences are strong and resilient. Belief-reporting sentences are taken to be a paradigm case of sentences that provoke anti-substitution intuitions. But these intuitions should be tested empirically. Aside from telling us whether or not the industry of accounting for anti-substitution intuitions has been built on a huge mistake, the comparison with simple sentence intuitions will be very useful. Results may be less clear-cut than one would expect.

B.2.3 Braun's account of belief reporting

David Braun's (1998) account of belief reporting bears important similarities to that suggested above. Braun is a Naïve Millian, who assigns Naïve Millian truth conditions to belief-reporting utterances. He explains anti-substitution intuitions about these utterances without invoking conversational implicatures, or indeed any intuition-matching propositions. Instead, he focuses on the guises under which belief-reporting propositions are apprehended and the evidence that we may have for the truth values that we assign to belief-reporting utterances.

Braun's central example, when it comes to explaining the intuitions of the enlightened, is that of Mary. Mary thinks that (10) is true and (10*) is false, despite the fact that she also knows (11) to be true. Braun's goal is to explain how it is that Mary might rationally hold this combination of beliefs.

(10) Hammurabi believes that Hesperus is visible in the evening.
(10*) Hammurabi believes that Phosphorus is visible in the evening.
(11) Hesperus is Phosphorus.

According to Braun (as to most Millians), Mary will grasp the proposition expressed by (10) and (10*) under different guises when she apprehends it via sentences (10) and (10*). Braun finds it convenient to discuss Mary's beliefs by provisionally adopting a mental sentence theory of belief. (He does not commit himself to the truth of such a view, nor does his explanation depend on it.) According to such a view, 'to believe a proposition is to have in one's head (in the right way) a mental sentence that expresses that proposition' (Braun 1998: 574). When a person is in such a state, the sentence in question is said to be in the person's *belief box*. Using this terminology, Braun claims that Mary has (10) in her belief box but does not have (10*) in her belief box. Indeed, she has (10**) in her belief box.

(10**) Hammurabi does not believe that Phosphorus is visible in the evening.

But this is clearly not enough: Braun also needs to explain how it is that Mary might rationally fail to make the inference from (10) and (11) to (10*). Braun's explanation depends on the thought that people may rationally fail to make even simple logical inferences. According to him, Mary may fail to make the inference in question simply because she has good reasons for thinking that (10) and (10**) are true. Her reasons may be, he suggests, so strong that she would be justified in rejecting the inference rather than giving up these beliefs. When this is the case, Mary may rationally assign different truth values to (10) and (10*) despite her knowledge that (11) is true.

Braun's account of belief-reporting intuitions has obvious similarities to that suggested earlier in this appendix in particular, (1) he draws on the idea that one may (quite reasonably) fail to make simple inferences simply because one has good reason to doubt that the inferences are correct; (2) he assigns a crucial role to the guises under which propositions are apprehended; and (3) he does not make use of intuition-matching propositions of any sort. Like the explanation I have been suggesting, Braun's explanation relies on processing considerations.

Braun's explanation and mine also have some dissimilarities, some merely apparent and some genuine. A first dissimilarity is that Braun's explanation makes use of a mental sentence theory of belief, and of belief boxes. But this is not a significant difference: Braun uses this theory merely as a helpful way of illustrating his approach, and he is not at all committed to it. His explanation in no way depends upon it. Somewhat more significantly, my explanation makes use of some claims about cognitive architecture that Braun does not, in particular the idea that groups of beliefs are stored separately from each other. This claim is by no means incompatible with Braun's account; he could well choose to make use of it. However, they do render the account at least somewhat distinct from his. Braun's view of belief reporting and the one suggested earlier in this appendix are, it seems to me, similar enough that acceptance of the psychological explanation for our intuitions about simple sentences can be used as an argument for Braun's view on belief-reporting.

References

Ammeson, J. (2002). 'The Lens of Time'. *World Traveller*, January, pp. 37–43.

Anderson, J. (1977). 'Memory for Information About Individuals'. *Memory & Cognition*, 5(4): 430–42.

——— and R. Hastie (1974). 'Individuation and Reference in Memory: Proper Names and Definite Descriptions'. *Cognitive Psychology*, 6: 495–514.

Bach, K. (1994). 'Conversational Impliciture'. *Mind and Language*, 9: 124–62.

——— (1999). 'The Myth of Conventional Implicature'. *Linguistics & Philosophy*, 22(4): 327–66.

——— (2001). 'You Don't Say?' *Synthese*, 128: 15–44.

——— (2002). 'Seemingly Semantic Intuitions', in J. K. Campbell, M. O'Rourke, and D. Shier (eds.), *Meaning and Truth: Investigations in Philosophical Semantics*. New York: Seven Bridges Press.

——— (2004). 'Pragmatics and the Philosophy of Language', in L. Horn and G. Ward (eds.), *Handbook of Pragmatics*. Oxford: Blackwell.

Barber, A. (2000). 'A Pragmatic Treatment of Simple Sentences'. *Analysis*, 60: 300–8.

Braun, D. (1998). 'Understanding Belief Reports'. *Philosophical Review*, 107: 555–95.

——— (2000). 'Russellianism and Psychological Generalizations'. *Nous*, pp. 203–36.

——— (2002). 'Cognitive Significance, Attitude Ascriptions, and Ways of Believing Propositions'. *Philosophical Studies*, 108: (65–81).

——— (2003). 'Review of Scott Soames's *Beyond Rigidity*', *Linguistics and Philosophy*, 26: 365–78.

——— and J. Saul (2002). 'Simple Sentences, Substitution, and Mistaken Evaluations'. *Philosophical Studies*: 1–41.

——— and T. Sider. (Forthcoming). 'Kripke's Revenge'. *Philosophical Studies*.

Carston, R. (1991). 'Implicature, Explicature, and Truth–Theoretic Semantics', in S. Davis (ed.), *Pragmatics*. New York: Oxford University Press.

——— (2002). *Thoughts and Utterances: The Pragmatics of Explicit Communication*. Oxford: Blackwell.

Cole, P. (1978). *Syntax and Semantics Vol. 9: Pragmatics*. London: Academic Press.

Crimmins, M. (1992). *Talk About Beliefs*. Cambridge, MA: MIT Press.

——— and J. Perry. (1989). 'The Prince and the Phone Booth'. *The Journal of Philosophy*, 86: 685–711.

Davis, W. (1998). *Implicature: Intention, Convention, and Principle in the Failure of Gricean Theory*. Cambridge: Cambridge University Press.

Erickson, T. D. and M. E. Mattson (1981). 'From Words to Meaning: A Semantic Illusion'. *Journal of Verbal Learning and Verbal Behavior*, 20: 540–51.

Evans, J. St. B. T., S. E. Newstead, and R. M. J. Byrne (1993). *Human Reasoning: The Psychology of Deduction*. Hove: Lawrence Erlbaum.

Forbes, G. (1990). 'The Indispensability of *Sinn*'. *The Philosophical Review*, 99: 535–63.

_____ (1993). 'Reply to Marks'. *Philosophical Studies*, 69: 281–95.

_____ (1997). 'How Much Substitutivity?'. *Analysis*, 57: 109–13.

_____ (1999). 'Enlightened Semantics for Simple Sentences.' *Analysis*, 59: 86–91.

_____ (2002). 'Intensionality'. *Proceedings of the Aristotelian Society Supplementartry Volume*, 76: 75–99.

_____ (2006). *Attitude Problems*. Oxford: Oxford University Press.

Frege, G. ([1892] 1970). 'On Sense and Reference', in P. Geach and M. Black (eds.), *Translations from the Philosophical Writings of Gottlob Frege*, 2nd edition. Oxford: Blackwell.

Green, M. (1998). 'Direct Reference and Implicature'. *Philosophical Studies*, 91: 61–90.

Grice, P. (1989). *Studies in the Way of Words*. Cambridge: Harvard University Press.

Hannon, B. and M. Daneman (2001). 'Susceptibility to Semantic Illusions: An Individual–Differences Perspective'. *Memory & Cognition*, 29: 449–61.

Horn, L. (1992). 'The Said and the Unsaid'. *Working Papers in Linguistics*, pp. 193–92.

Kamas, E. N., L. M. Reder, and M. S. Ayers (1996). 'Partial Matching in the Moses Illusion: Response Bias Not Sensitivity'. *Memory & Cognition*, 24: 687–99.

Kripke, S. (1972). *Naming and Necessity*. Cambridge, MA: Harvard University Press.

_____ (1988). 'A Puzzle About Belief', in N. Salmon and S. Soames (eds.), *Propositions and Attitudes*. Oxford: Oxford University Press, pp. 102–48.

Levinson, S. C. (1983). *Pragmatics*. Cambridge: Cambridge University Press.

_____ (2000). *Presumptive Meanings: The Theory of Generalized Conversational Implicature*. Cambridge, MA: MIT Press.

Moore, J. (1999). 'Saving Substitutivity in Simple Sentences'. *Analysis*, pp. 91–105.

_____ (2000). 'Did Clinton Lie?' *Analysis*, 60: 250–4.

Moos, J. (1997). 'It's a bird! It's a plane! It's a costume change!'. Available at: http://www.cnn.com/SHOWBIZ/9703/12/superman/

Neale, S. (1990). *Descriptions*. Cambridge: MIT University Press.

_____ (1992). 'Paul Grice and the Philosophy of Language'. *Linguistics and Philosophy*, 15: 509–59.

_____ (2002). 'Pragmatism and Binding', in Z. Szabo (ed.), *Semantics versus Pragmatics*. Oxford: Oxford University Press, pp. 165–285.

Oakhill, J., P. N. Johnson-Laird, and A. Garnham (1989). 'Believability and Syllogistic Reasoning'. *Cognition*, 31(2): 117–40.

Pitt, D. (2001). 'Alter Egos and Their Names'. *Journal of Philosophy*, 98: 531–52.

Predelli, S. (1999). 'Saul, Salmon, and Superman'. *Analysis*, 59(2): 113–16.

_____ (2001). 'Art, Bart, and Superman'. *Analysis*, 61(4): 310–13.

_____ (2004). 'Superheroes and their Names'. *American Philosophical Quarterly*, 41(2).

Recanati, F. (1991). 'The Pragmatics of What is Said', in S. Davis (ed.), *Pragmatics: A Reader*. New York: Oxford University Press.

_____ (1993). *Direct Reference: From Language to Thought*. Oxford: Blackwell.

_____ (2001). 'What is Said'. *Synthese*, 128: 75–91.

Reder, L. M. and G. Kusbit (1991). 'Locus of the Moses Illusion: Imperfect Encoding, Retrieval, or Match?' *Journal of Memory and Language*, 30: 385–406.

Reimer, M. (1991). 'Demonstratives, Demonstrations, and Demonstrata'. *Philosophical Studies*, 63: 187–202.

Richard, M. (1990). *Propositional Attitudes: An Essay on Thoughts and How We Ascribe Them*. Cambridge: Cambridge University Press.

_____ (1993). 'Sense, Necessity and Belief', *Philosophical Studies*, 69: 243–63.

Sadock. J. (1978). 'On Testing for Conversational Implicature', in P. Cole (ed.), *Syntax and Semantics Vol. 9: Pragmatics*. London: Academic Press.

Salmon, N. (1981). *Reference and Essence*. Princeton, NJ: Princeton University Press.

_____ (1986). *Frege's Puzzle*. Cambridge, MA: MIT Press.

_____ (1989). 'Illogical Belief', *Philosophical Perspectives 3: Philosophy of Mind and Action Theory*, 243–85.

_____ (2003). 'Naming, Necessity, and Beyond', *Mind*, 112: 447–92.

Saul, J. (1992). 'Still an Attitude Problem'. *Linguistics and Philosophy*, 16.

_____ (1997*a*). 'Substitution and Simple Sentences'. *Analysis*, 57: 102–8.

_____ (1997*b*). 'Reply to Forbes'. *Analysis*, 57: 114–18.

_____ (1998). 'The Pragmatics of Attitude Ascription'. *Philosophical Studies*, 92: 363–98.

_____ (1999*a*). 'The Best of Intentions: Ignorance, Idiosyncrasy, and Belief Reporting'. *Canadian Journal of Philosophy*, 19: 29–48.

_____ (1999*b*). 'The Road to Hell: Intentions and Propositional Attitude Ascription.' *Mind & Language*, 14: 356–75.

_____ (1999*c*). 'Substitution, Simple Sentences, and Sex Scandals.' *Analysis*, 59: 106–12.

_____ (2000). 'Did Clinton Say Something False?' *Analysis*, 60: 255–7.

_____ (2001). 'Critical Study of Davis'. *Conversational Implicature*. *Noûs*, 35: 630–41.

Saul, J.(2002*a*). 'Speaker Meaning, What is Said, and What is Implicated' *Nous*, 36(2): 228–48.

Saul, J. (2002*b*). 'What is Said and Psychological Reality: Grice's Project and Relevance Theorists' Criticisms'. *Linguistics and Philosophy*, 25: 347–72.

Schiffer, S. (1987). 'The "Fido"-Fido theory of Belief', in J. Tomberlin (ed.), *Philosophical Perspectives 1: Metaphysics.* Atascadero: Ridgeview, pp. 455–80.

———(1992). 'Belief Ascription'. *Journal of Philosophy* LXXXIX, pp. 499–521.

Sider, T. (1995). 'Three Problems for Richard's Theory of Belief Ascription'. *Canadian Journal of Philosophy*, 25: 487–514.

Soames, S. (1988). 'Direct Reference, Propositional Attitudes, and Semantic Content', in N. Salmon and S. Soames (eds.), *Propositions and Attitudes.* Oxford: Oxford University Press, pp. 197–239.

———(1995). 'Beyond Singular Propositions?' *Canadian Journal of Philosophy*, 25: 515–50.

———(2002). *Beyond Rigidity: The Unfinished Semantic Agenda of* Naming and Neccessity. Oxford: Oxford University Press.

Sperber, D. and D. Wilson (1986). *Relevance: Communication and Cognition.* Cambridge, MA: Harvard University Press.

——— ——— (1995). *Relevance: Communication and Cognition*, 2nd edn. Oxford: Blackwell.

Thau, M. (2002). *Consciousness and Cognition.* Oxford: Oxford University Press.

Wason, P. (1966). 'Reasoning', in B. M. Foss (ed.), *New Horizons in Psychology.* Harmondsworth: Pelican, pp. 135–51.

Wettstein, H. (1984). 'How to Bridge the Gap Between Meaning and Reference'. *Synthese*, 58: 63–84.

Wilson, D. and Sperber, D. (1981). 'On Grice's Theory of Conversation', in P. Werth (ed.), *Conversation and Discourse.* London: Croom Helm.

Zimmerman, T. E. (2005). 'What's in Two Names?' *Journal of Semantics*, 23: 53–96.

Index